Kavan

Meditations of the Heart

Written by
Reb Moshe Steinerman

Edited by Elise Teitelbaum

Ilovetorah Jewish Outreach Network

iloveTorah Jewish Publishing
First Published 2018
ISBN # 978-1-947706-01-9

Editor: Elise Teitelbaum
Artwork by Boris Shapiro
Book Formatted by Rabbi Benyamin Fleischman

Ilovetorah.com is a non-profit organization. Please help support our Jewish Outreach with your donation. The books are sold at very low costs and it is a great mitzvah to help support ilovetorah projects. Contact Reb Moshe to help at moshe@ilovetorah.com

Dear Reader,

Ilovetorah Jewish Outreach is an online, non-profit organization, where books and *Torah* classes are available at low cost. Therefore, we appreciate your donation to help Rabbi Moshe Steinerman, and ilovetorah.com, in order to help them continue their work on behalf of the Jewish people. We also ask that you pass on these books to others once you are finished with them.

Thank you,
Reb Moshe Steinerman
www.ilovetorah.com
Donations
www.ilovetorah.com/donations

ABOUT THE AUTHOR

Rabbi Moshe Steinerman grew up as a religious Jew on the hillsides of Maryland. In his teens he roamed the mountains, taking photographs and speaking to *Hashem*, inclining toward the *chassidus* of Breslev but maintaining closeness to the *Litvish* style of learning. He studied in a Baltimore *yeshiva*, Ner Yisrael, married and then moved to Lakewood, New Jersey, where he wrote <u>Kavanos Halev</u> with the blessing of HaRav Malkiel Kotler Shlita, *Rosh Yeshiva* of Beis Medresh Gevoah.

After establishing one of the first Jewish outreach websites, ilovetorah.com, in 1996, Reb Moshe made *aliyah* to Tzfat in 2003 and helped to return thousands of English speaking Jews to Judaism, through his numerous Jewish videos, audio shiurim and outreach work. His teachings and stories of *tzaddikim* became popular among Jews around the world, from every background. His learning experience includes the completion of both Talmud Bavli and Yerushalmi as well as other important works.

In 2012 Reb Moshe and his family moved to Jerusalem.

Some of his other books are <u>Tikkun</u> <u>Shechinah</u>, <u>Tovim</u> <u>Meoros</u> (Glimpse of Light), <u>Chassidus</u> <u>Kabbalah</u> & <u>Meditation</u>, <u>Yom</u> <u>Leyom</u> (Day by Day), <u>Pesukei</u> <u>Torah</u> (Passages of Torah), <u>Prayers</u> <u>of</u> <u>the</u> <u>Heart</u>, <u>Pathways</u> <u>of</u> <u>the</u> <u>Righteous</u>, <u>A</u> <u>Journey into Holiness, and The True Intentions of the</u> <u>Baal Shem Tov</u>.

In Memory of my father Shlomo Zavel Ben Yaakov ZT'L
Menachem Ben Ruvein ZT'L
And all the great souls of our people

I grew up in a house filled with the *Torah* learning of my father, who studied most of the day. Although there were no Jews in this remote part of Maryland, my father was a man of *chesed* to all people and was known for his brilliance in *Torah* scholarship.

Dedicated to my wife Rochel
and to my children Shlomo Nachman, Yaakov Yosef, Gedalya Aharon Tzvi,
Ester Rivka, Yeshiya Michel, Dovid Shmuel, Eliyahu Yisrael
May it bring forth the light of your neshamos.

RABBINICAL APPROVALS / HASKAMAH

בס״ד

RABBI DOVID B. KAPLAN
RABBI OF WEST NEW YORK
5308 PALISADE AVENUE • WEST NEW YORK, NJ 07093
201-867-6859 • WESTNEWYORKSHUL@GMAIL.COM

דוד ברוך הלוי קאפלאן
רב ואב״ד דק״ק
וועסט ניו יארק

י' שבט ה'תשע"ז / February 6, 2017

Dear Friends,

Shalom and Blessings!

For approximately twenty years I have followed the works of Rabbi Moshe Steinerman, Shlit"a, a pioneer in the use of social media to encourage people and bring them closer to G-d.

Over the years Rabbi Steinerman has produced, and made public at no charge, hundreds of videos sharing his Torah wisdom, his holy stories, and his touching songs. Rabbi Steinerman has written a number of books, all promoting true Jewish Torah spirituality. Rabbi Steinerman's works have touched many thousands of Jews, and even spirituality-seeking non-Jews, from all walks of life and at all points of the globe.

Rabbi Steinerman is a tomim (pure-hearted one) in the most flattering sense of the word.

I give my full approbation and recommendation to all of Rabbi Steinerman's works.

I wish Rabbi Steinerman much success in all his endeavors.

May G-d bless Rabbi Moshe Steinerman, his wife, Rebbetzin Rochel Steinerman, and their beautiful children; and may G-d grant them health, success, and nachas!

With blessings,

Rabbi Dovid B. Kaplan

בע"ה

RABBI ARYEH MALKIEL KOTLER
BETH MEDRASH GOVOHA
LAKEWOOD, N.J. 08701

ארי' מלכיאל קוטלר
בית מדרש גבוה
לייקוואוד, נ. דז.

ב' אלול תשס"ב

הנה יען הן הספרן לאה, קעה כל להרא' ירוא שאים הר' יראה הנו
רבה טבי', ובמס' בפאה, מרעומר ב מסן שבא'ינ החושים, והגל הפלא'
האסבת את רשעה שלמן, וע' אמר לכר'ו כבבא אל דך ה' אל את הה א'נ את
ורא.צ לכבם גת לךם אוהר לגם לאה, לישאל כא" שבה כן גלו" טובה ה
ונו' היו לרא לישה תן אלה ודל אשה רבתן לו רשה לנן לישר/ שלו
לאתה אע אר' ודל ובתלם ולה רמן ה' לכם לב לדה ודו' אל והיין שלא
גאצ'ו חלשאם רוחן'ם לעא'ג יראאו

אלברון ןפלו': לאאה אפה רעא א?א אבוטב' עד התוה לעיגוולוד יפן
בשוהבד אשה ש?רון פ'לון אלס' אטר גבר אלאתאת' גבוא בהלבאתו לפוב
רתורום לאשה ולאאונה וירשו אאר? לאור סכר בוכה הבקוכבת רבם
בוונה הלד אשר אתתלגום פלא'א' אר.ספר ג'ובר לולות שאום
אוקמו' ופאבא הפם שלבבן ורה אלא אך הפ' הגל וסרא ל הקבוטום
והלב'ת אל סלא'ג' אבוב'ם אל הראש' ורה שבפה לה'ו' רבר
שמען אאת' ס'כנפ כפ'ן אלב יבוקו אעוןגאו לתבק'ל אוה ולהבה'ה

בכוה לכבוד התורה
באלו הם אך

Approval of the Baila Rebbe of New York / Miami/ Betar Israel

הובא לפני גליונות בעניני קירוב רחוקים לקרב אחינו בני ישראל אל
אביהם שבשמים, כידוע מהבעש"ט זיע"א שאמר "אימתי קאתי מר
לכשיפוצו מעינותיך חוצה" ואפריון נמטי"ה להאי גברא יקרא מיקירי
צפת עיה"ק תובב"א כמע"כ מוהר"ר משה שטיינרמן שליט"א אשר כבר
עוסק רבות בשנים לקרב רחוקים לתורה וליהדות, וכעת מוציא לאור
ספר בשם "כוונת הלב" וראיתי דברים נחמדים מאוד וניכר מתוך
הדברים שהרב בעל המחבר - אהבת השי"ת ואהבת התורה וישראל
בלבבו, ובטחוני כי הספר יביא תועלת גדולה לכל עם ישראל.

ויה"ר שיזכה לבוא לגומרה ברוב פאר והדר ונזכה לגאולתן של ישראל
בב"א.

בכבוד רב:

אהרן שלמה חיים אליעזר
בלאאאו"ר בלללהה"ה אביאלא

Rabbi M. Lebovits

Grand Rabbi of
Nikolsburg

53 Decatur Avenue
Spring Valley, N.Y. 10977

יוסף יחיאל מיכל
לעבאוויטש
ניקלשבורג

מאנסי - ספרינג וואלי, נ. י.

בעזהשי"ת

בשורותי אלו באתי להעיד על מעשה אומן, מופלא מופלג בהפלגת חכמים ונבונים,
ירא וחרד לדבר ה', ומשתוקק לקרב לבות ישראל לאביהם שבשמים,
ה"ה הרב **משה שטיינערמאן** שליט"א בעיה"ק צפת תובב"א

שעלה בידו להעלות על הספר דברים נפלאים שאסף מספרים הקדושים, בענין אהבה
אחוה שלום וריעות, לראות מעלות חברינו ולא חסרונם, זעי"ז להיות נמנעים מדברי
ריבות ומחלוקת, ולתקן עון שנאת חנם אשר בשביל זה נחרב בית מקדשינו
ותפארתינו, וכמשאחז"ל (רש"י ובמדרש רבה ש ב') על ויחן שם ישראל, שניתנה תורה באופן
שחנו שם כאיש אחד בלב אחד.

וניכר בספר כי עמל ויגע הרבה להוציא מתח"י דבר נאה ומתוקן, ע"כ אף ידי תכון
עמו להוציאו לאור עולם, ויהי רצון שהפין ה' בידו יצליח, ויברך ה' חילו ופועל ידו
תרצה, שיברך על המוגמר להגדיל תורה ולהאדירה ולהפיצו בקרב ישראל, עד ביאת
גוא"צ בב"א

א"ד הכותב לכבוד התורה ומרביציה.
י"ט חשון תשס"ו

Rabbi Abraham Y. S. Friedman
161 Maple Avenue #C Spring Valley NY 10977
Tel: 845-425-5043 Fax: 845-425-8045

רב דביהמ"ד אמר"י ספ"ר קאמאדא
וראש כולל חאר"י

בעזהשי"ת

ישפות השם החיים והשלו', לכבוד ידידי מאז ומקדם מיקירי קרתא דירושלים יראה שלם, זוכה ומזכה אחרים, להיות דבוק באלקינו, ה"ה הר"ר משה שטיינרמאן שליט"א.

שמחתי מאוד לשמוע ממך, מאתר רחוק וקירוב הלבבות, בעסק תורתך הקדושה ועבודתך בלי לאות, וכה יעזור ה' להלאה ביתר שאת ויתר עז. והנה שלחת את הספר שלקטת בעניני דביקות בה', לקרב לבבות בני ישראל לאבינו שבשמים בשפת אנגלית, אבל דא עקא השפת לא ידענו, ע"כ לא זכיתי לקרותו, ע"כ א"א לי ליתן הסכמה פרטי על ספרך, ובכלל קיבלתי על עצמי שלא ליתן הסכמות, ובפרט כשאין לי פנאי לקרות הספר מתחלתו עד סופו, אבל בכלליות זכרתי לך חסד נעוריך, היאך הי' המתיקות שלך בעבודת השם פה בעירינו, ובנועם המדות, וחזקה על חבר שאינו מוציא מתחת ידו דבר שאינו מתוקן, ובפרט שכל מגמתך להרבות כבוד שמים, שבוודאי סייעתא דשמיא ילוך כל ימיך לראות רב נחת מיוצ"ח ומפרי ידיך, שתתקבל הספר בסבר פנים יפות אצל אחינו בני ישראל שמדברים בשפת האנגלית שיתקרבו לאבינו שבשמים ולהדבק בו באמת כאות נפשך, ולהרבות פעלים לתורה ועבודה וקדושה בדביקות עם מדות טובות, בנייחותא נייחא בעליונים ונייחא בתחתונים עד ביאת גואל צדק בב"א.

כ"ד ידידך השמח בהצלחתך ובעבודתך
אברהם יחזקאל שרגא פרידמאן
אמר"י קאמאדא

בס"ד

ברכת חבירך

אור ליום שלישי שנכפל בו כי טוב ר"ח ניסן תשס"ז לפ"ק
לכבוד ידיד נפשי ירא וחרד לדבר ד' שהכרתיו מאז
לא' ממבקשי ה', הרב ר' משה שטיינרמאן שליט"א

אחדשה"ט, שמחתי מאד לראות העלים לתרופה שמעלת
כבודו נתן לי לעיין בהם, ואף שרחוק אני מאד מלכתוב אפי'
מעין הסכמה, מ"מ מתוך אהבה מקלקלת השורה, אכתוב
לו קצת דברי הערכה, בהם שמכיר אני מדלה שכוונתו
לשמים, ומתוך שלמדתי אתך משך זמן בחברותא ספרי יראה
וחסידות, ומכיר אני היטב את עומק פנימיות רצונך הטוב,
מה גודל שמחתי באמת ששמעתי שהספר "כוונת הלב"
כבר מוכן לדפוס, והצצתי קצת פה וקצת פה, וראיתי שכולה
מליאה עצות והדרכות האיך להתקרב לבורא כל העולמים
בלב שלם, ויודע אני גודל כשרונך לעשות בעלי תשובה ולקרבם
לתורה ומצות כפי שכבר פעל מע"כ הרבה גדולות ונצורות
בזה, ועוד ידו נטויה בעזה"י ביתר שאת ויתר עז להרבות פעלים
בדרכים שונים בקירוב וחינוך לבבות נשברות שתועים מן הדרך
ה', לקרבם לתורה ומצות ולהעלותם למסילה העולה בית ד', ויה"ר
שמע"כ הרבה יצליח לזכות את הרבים למעלה מן המשוער,
ולהוסיף אור וחינוך ובפרט בימים טרופים כאלו השם ישמרנו, שעם
ישראל זקוקים לרחמי שמים מרובים, ולהיות מן הזוכים והמזכים
עד שיזכו בנו בקרוב ממש לשמוע קול שופר במהרה ויבואו
לציון ברינה. ונזכה עוד בשנה הזו לאכול מן הזבחים ומן הפסחים
ושם נשיר לך שיר חדש על גאולתינו ועל פדות נפשינו, בב"א אמן

מאת אוהבך נצח בלב ונפש חפיצה
יששכר דוב רומפלער
מחס לערב ורובו - בדיני היתר תיקון עירובין
פה ציה"ק צפת תובב"א.

INTRODUCTION TO KAVANOS HALEV

As the era of the *Moshiach's* coming approaches, thousands of Jews are seeking out the depths of *Torah* like never before. They study the great works of the Chassidic *rebbes* and *talmedei chachamim*, with the intention of applying this proven advice to their lives. This book, <u>Kavanos Halev</u> teaches a practical, yet advanced approach in *avodas Hashem*, based on the teachings of our Sages.

This *sefer* is written with the intention of helping every Jew reach his or her true spiritual potential. The keys to accomplishing purity of mind will be explained in the following chapters. In each chapter, I have included some of my own personal thoughts, *chiddushim*, and numerous quotes from *gedolei* Torah.

Rebbe Nachman says that a delightful story has the ability to touch a person, kindling the fire of the soul. <u>Kavanos Halev</u> combines powerful teachings from our *mesorah* and stories of *tzaddikim*. Based on the topics addressed, each chapter is followed by a brief prayer to *HaShem* for success.

To find holiness in the mundane is no easy task. We must have patience with ourselves and with our generation. Advice from sages can be found in the *sifrei kodesh*; but to find one that speaks to you, answering your troubles with practical advice, is rare. Finally, a *sefer* is available to answer the cries of *Klal Yisrael* in this generation and to uplift and bring relief to those feeling spiritually unfulfilled.

TABLE OF CONTENTS

CHAPTER 1: AVODAS HASHEM, SERVING HASHEM

"Shivisi HaShem l'negdi samid - I have placed the L-RD before me constantly." (Psalms 16:8)

We should always be conscious of the purpose of our existence. Should we forget for even a moment, our connection to the *Shechinah*[1] could be lost. Impurity and material distraction, tempting us to waste our short and valuable time in this life, surround us. Each of us decides how to make use of *HaShem's* gifts, either to our advantage or disadvantage, through one of those gifts, that of free will. It is not always easy to choose the correct path, especially when doing what is right often involves much effort and arduous work. One cannot merely coast through life without examining the options and decisions before him. Every one of us has the power to come closer to *HaShem*. We are like programmers who create a means by which the computer can perform specific tasks. The programmer creates a flow chart that starts at the beginning and follows a path based on decisions made along the way, abiding by specific rules. To program our lives, we do the same thing. Our rules are the *mitzvos.*[2]

The wisest of all men, Shlomo HaMelech, wrote in the first chapter of Proverbs, "The beginning of wisdom is the fear of *HaShem.*"[3] Rav Elazar teaches, "If a man desires to serve his Master, where should he begin? In 'Fear of Heaven', from where the ascent to Heaven commences."[4] According to Rabbi Elazar, "The Holy One praised is He said, 'The whole world would not have been created if not for him [who fears G-d][5]. The importance placed on fearing one's Creator is quite apparent. Not only is it

---

1 Divine Presence
2 Commandments
3 Proverbs 1:7
4 Zohar 3:56b
5 Ayin Yakkov Berachos 6

the beginning of wisdom; it is also the beginning of true life as a Jew.

What is fear of *Hashem*? Is it a single entity, lacking dimension, or is it multi-faceted? Fear is comprised of two separate but similar components: Fear of punishment and awe and respect for *Hashem*. Fear of punishment from *Hashem* is not the same as from parents. A child learns to fear his parents. When he hits his brother in self-defense, he gets a little *potch*[6] from his parent or is sent to his room. While in his room he gets to review the incident and examine his actions, the siblings, and the parents. In his mind, he was justified to hit his brother. He doesn't understand why he deserved punishment when he was merely reacting to his brother's initiation of a fight. When his parents punish him immediately, the child learns to avoid that reaction in the future.

Unlike the parent who teaches that every action has a direct consequence (reward or punishment), *Hashem* might mete out an *onesh*[7] at any moment, immediately after the infraction or at some future time. *Hashem* hides the direct correlation between action and reward or punishment, so we can exercise free will. If we always stubbed our toe immediately after getting angry, it would be evident that *Hashem* runs the world. We would go through life as puppets rather than intelligent beings able to understand and use free choice.

As adults, we try our hardest and think we are doing the right thing, but we feel as if we also receive a little *potch* from *Hashem*. Just when we think we are doing everything expected of us, the car breaks down or we accidentally cut ourselves with a knife. We then look at what happened and become angry with the auto mechanic who did not properly repair the car, or we blame whoever left the knife out. Do we ever check if we're at fault? Often, when something goes awry, our first question is 'What did I do to deserve this?' Only when we calm down, we analyze where our *midos*[8] or service of *Hashem* are lacking. We try to make sure that we do the right things to avoid *Hashem's* punishment. We do so to avoid pain, inconvenience, and distress. Sometimes it's not so easy to see the relationship between our actions and our unfortunate circumstances. We must keep in mind that *Hashem* sees our every action, thought and emotion. "They are the eyes of *Hashem*, which scan the entire earth."[9] If our thought is on Torah learning, fear of *HaShem*, or a *mitzvah*, then we are in sync with *HaShem*. Without fearing *HaShem* always, our thoughts might lead us to sinful actions and judgment.

Rebbe Nachman teaches that every night, when the sun goes down, *HaShem* judges every person. This process ends at *chatzos*, around

---

6 Spank
7 Punishment
8 Character traits
9 Zechariah 4:10

midnight. If a person sinned against a law or any of the commandments, the sin is brought before *HaShem* in the early evening hours. A person must judge daily all his actions and confess his wrongdoings to *HaShem*.[10] "When there is no judgment below, there is judgment above."[11] If a person wants to experience a taste of the *Or HaGanuz* (the hidden light), Torah mysteries from the future world, he must elevate the character trait of fear to its source. This is done through self-judgment. By following this, all false fear is removed and only pure *yiras HaShem* - fear of *HaShem* - remains.[12] "You should never fear anything except *HaShem*. If ever you begin to feel afraid of anything, remember the great fear that is due to *HaShem*. Throughout the day, fill your entire consciousness with this sense of awe. It will help you to pray with all your strength, to utter the words with such force that they are like thunderbolts! You will hear the words that are on your lips. This is the way to achieve true joy and to perform the *mitzvos* with a joy derived from the *mitzvos* themselves. You will attain the understanding of how to nullify all harsh decrees even after the decrees have been made, *Hashem* forbid. To achieve these levels, you must combine your fear of Heaven with love. A person's main strength lies in the love he has for *Hashem*. Nevertheless, fear must come first."[13]

The *tzaddik* Rabbi Levi Yitzchak of Berditchev possessed holiness like a *seraph*, a fiery angel. It is said that, when food was brought before him to eat, he made a blessing with such fervor and such a great fire of devotion that he would end up in one corner of the room and the food in the other.[14] A great rabbi learned Torah so vibrantly that awe of *HaShem* became a part of his essence. Wine was poured three times for the *kiddush*[15] of *rebbe* Mordechai of Chernobyl. Each time he tried to lift the cup he trembled so violently that the wine spilled. When he finally succeeded in saying the blessings, he was asked why he had trembled so much. He answered: "As the cup of wine was being poured, I meditated before Whom I was standing. I was struck by the awesomeness of *HaShem* and could not help but tremble."[16]

In the Talmud, Rabbah bar Rav Huna said, "One who has Torah but not fear of Heaven is like a treasurer who has been given the inner keys, but not the outer ones. How is he to enter?" Rabbi Yannai called out, "Woe to him who has no courtyard, but has made a gate to it."[17] The Torah is the

---

10 Learn how to do this in the Hisbodidus chapter.
11 Devarim Rabbah, 5:4
12 Likutey Maharan #15
13 Lekutey Eztos, Awe and Devotion
14 Seder ha-Dorot ha-Chadash, p. 36
15 The blessing made over wine on the Sabbath and holy days before the meal, to sanctify the day
16 From My Fathers *Shabbos* Table, Meditation
17 *Shabbos* 31a-b

only gate through which one can enter true fear of *Hashem*. Rav Judah said, "The Holy One blessed be He, created His world only that men should fear Him... and *HaShem* hath done it, that men should fear before Him."[18]

To incorporate fear of Heaven, sometimes you must contemplate your own purpose and what lies before you. Rabbi Akiva Ben Mahalel would say, "Reflect upon three things and you will never come to sin: Know from where you came, to where you are going, and before Whom you are destined to give an accounting. 'From where you came' - from a putrid drop; 'to where you are going' - to a place of dust, maggots, and worms; and before Whom you are destined to give an accounting' - before the King of Kings, the Holy One, blessed be He."[19]

We sin most often when we lack fear of *HaShem*. To guard against this, we must concentrate our efforts. Rabbi Yosef Caro placed fear of *HaShem* first when he wrote the *Shulchan Aruch*.[20] Explaining the *Shulchan Aruch*, the Chofetz Chaim says, "One must picture to himself always, that he is standing before *HaShem*, may He be blessed, for the Holy One, blessed be He, fills the entire universe with His glory."[21] We do not emphasize this concept enough today. How can one completely bond with *HaShem* without incorporating into our daily lives the concept of standing before His glory?

When we battle our *Yetzer Hara*[22] we should be more afraid of the disappointment that *HaShem* will have with us if we give in to the temptation, than the consequences we will bear due to our actions. We all have mortal parents who raised us, and we endeavor not to let them down. We want to give them reasons to be proud of us and to *shep nachas*[23] over our accomplishments. How much more do we want this for our Heavenly Father. If we fail Him, His disappointment inflicts us more than the greatest torture in *Gehinnom*.[24] Our real affliction comes from having to see how we failed as servants of a King full only of love and *chesed*[25] for His creations. To reach this level, we must analyze the *mitzvos* and their intent. Many of our *mitzvos* that deal with relationships between people help us relate to *HaShem*. A good example is the *mitzvah* of *kibbud av v'aim* - honoring one's father and mother. Why did *HaShem* create parents? You might think it's obvious that parents are needed to care for and guide a child. However, if He chose, *HaShem* could have created people to be immediately self-sufficient. The role of a parent is to impart respect and fear of authority

---

18 Ecclesiastes 3,14
19 Pirkei Avos 3:1
20 The Code of Jewish Law
21 Mishna Berurah
22 Evil inclination
23 Derive pleasure
24 Final punishment and purification
25 Kindness

and, ultimately, *HaShem*. If children are taught that they must listen when their parents tell them 'no' when they are older and *HaShem* says no, they will be equipped with self-control.

There are two emotions that define our obligations to *HaShem* in our relationship with the Creator. We must love Him, and we must revere Him. The two are not separate and distinct. Within love there must be a sense of awe and reverence; within fear, there must also be an outpouring of love. A person could attempt to serve *HaShem* only out of fear, but his service would be limited. When a person adds the love of *HaShem* to his fear, this brings him to a new *madreiga*.[26] You can do anything in life without loving it but, when your heart is not in what you do, the job lacks sincerity. When *HaShem* created man, He did so out of the greatest love for what we would become. The only way to come close to *HaShem* is to return this love by serving Him to the fullest degree of our ability and understanding.

The Baal Shem Tov once invited his students: "Come; let us learn a lesson in the love of *HaShem*." They followed him to a nearby field where a shepherd tended his flock. Suddenly, the shepherd lifted his voice towards Heaven and exclaimed, "Dear *HaShem*, my love for you has no bounds! I will express my love by jumping back and forth across this small pond." After jumping back and forth for some time, he exclaimed heavenward again: "What can I offer you to prove my deep love for you, oh *HaShem*? Here... I have a coin in my pocket. I will give it to you." The shepherd took the coin and cast it heavenward. Some versions of this story relate that the coin did not descend.[27]

Love and fear of *HaShem* are the vehicles through which we are elevated to higher levels of spiritual greatness. We are only human beings and, for some of us, trying to avoid punishment or gain a reward is the only reason we perform *mitzvos*. We must strive for truth and work hard to reach higher levels of spirituality where those who serve *HaShem* out of love and fear, seeking nothing in return, dwell.

"You are to serve *HaShem* with both fear and joy. These are 'two friends that do not separate [from each other].' Fear without joy brings depression. It is inappropriate to feel anguished in serving *HaShem*; you should always be joyful."[28] Fear on its own can lead to gloominess and dejection. Joy on its own leads to carelessness and frivolity. The Zohar says, "When a man comes to serve his Master he should do so first in fear, and through that fear, he will afterward perform the precepts of the Law in joy."[29] Fear and joy help a person to have proper thoughts. The Zohar says, "Man is identical with his thought."[30] The Baal Shem Tov further explains:

---

26 Spiritual level
27 A Journey Into Holiness p. 34
28 Tzava'as Harivash 110
29 Zohar 3:56a

"Wherever the person's will and thoughts are, that is where he is himself."[31] Therefore, we have a responsibility to be in the right place with our thoughts, especially seeing that "*HaShem* knows the thoughts of man."[32]

Anyone can serve a king, but the servants who do so out of love are favored. In the same way, it is not the complicated actions and *hanhagos*[33] that *HaShem* yearns for us to perform; rather it is the *mitzvos* with love that He seeks. A humble man who puts his heart into everything he does, even the simplest of actions, shows *HaShem* genuine intent. Sometimes we get caught up in complexities and we forget the simple, pure love and *avodah*[34] that *HaShem* truly desires from us.

A pious Jew was praying alongside the road when a prince came along and met him. The prince greeted the man but, since he was praying, the Jew ignored the prince and did not return the greeting. The prince waited angrily until the man ended his prayer and then rebuked him, "If I would have cut off your head, would you then have answered me?" The Jew began to explain in the form of a parable why he chose to continue praying. "If you had been standing before a mortal king and a common man saluted you, would you have answered him?" The prince responded that he would not. "If you would have spoken to the person, what would the king have done to you?" asked the Jew. "He would surely have ordered my head to be cut off with a sword," replied the prince. The pious Jew, sensing victory, responded, "Behold, if this is what you would have done when you stood before a mortal king who is with us today and tomorrow may be in his grave, how much more care do I need to take when standing before the Supreme King of Kings, *HaShem*, Who lives and endures forever to all eternity!" The prince was appeased and sent the pious man home untouched.[35]

When a person truly loves someone, he is willing to do anything to make the loved one happy. There is no greater feeling than being close to someone you truly love. At times we might unintentionally hurt the feelings of people who love us. If the love is strong, it will usually not be destroyed. However, if the love is weak and not real, it could shatter.

The love *HaShem* has for us is so strong that it cannot be broken. Even if we are not worthy, He constantly gives to us out of a love that is whole and true. It is taught in Tomer Devorah that *HaShem* suffers great humiliation because of us. Even when one sins, *HaShem* continues to send His sustenance to that person. If *chalila*[36] He did not the person would cease

---

30 Tikkuney Zohar 21:63
31 Keter Shem Tov
32 Psalms 94:11
33 Stringencies
34 Worship
35 Ayin Yaakov 32

to exist, but *HaShem* is slow to anger and has tremendous patience for us. He gives us many chances to repent and continues to nourish us. If one would recognize this, would he ever sin and cause *HaShem* such degradation? The Chazon Ish once remarked, 'The only pleasure for me is to do the will of *HaShem*. I could suffer no greater hurt than to be ensnared by sin. My teachers taught me that, before any move, one must consult the *Shulchan Aruch*, the Code of Jewish Law... That is all I have in this world.'[37]

There is no excuse for intentionally hurting someone who is close to you; this especially holds true to our Creator. Unfortunately, we all struggle with this and usually hurt those about whom we care the most. Let us try to reflect before taking actions that could lead us to sin or to hurt a fellow Jew. If we would take the time to think before acting we could save everyone, including ourselves, so much hurt.

HaShem gives us so much and all He asks in return from us is to do a few *mitzvos* and study Torah. One of the greatest *mitzvos* is learning Torah, as we say in morning *berochos*[38] "The study of Torah is equal to all of them [*mitzvos* for which the main reward will be given in the World-to-Come]". Shlomo HaMelech taught that the Torah is "A Tree of Life to those who hold fast to it."[39] A person's devotion to the study of Torah is the key to his ability to properly fear *HaShem*. According to *Chazal*, the Torah is the blueprint of Creation.[40] As our manual for the performance of the commandments, it teaches us how to live and act as Jews. Without Torah, there is no fear of *HaShem* in one's life. We learn, "This Torah shall not depart from your mouth."[41]

When you borrow money from the bank, it charges you interest and does not reward you when you pay it back. *HaShem* gives us our bodies as a loan to perform His commandments; when you repay the loan, He gives you more than any worldly reward. *HaShem* gives us a glimpse of His glory, which is the most precious gift. The righteous say, "One moment in this world is worth the entire world to come."[42] When one goes to the next world, it is no longer possible to perform any *mitzvos*. *HaShem* rewards everyone in the next world, but a person cannot add to his slate of virtuous deeds. These beautiful *neshomas*[43] would do anything just to acquire one simple *mitzvah* that we have the opportunity to perform every day. To them, rising from one spiritual level to the next is like the difference between black and white. *Chazal* teaches that in the next world a person is

---

36 Heaven Forbid
37 Kovetz Igros Chazon Ish 1:153
38 Blessings
39 Proverbs 3:18
40 Our sages
41 Joshua 8:10
42 Pirkei Avos 4:22
43 Souls

embarrassed to look in the eye of someone on a higher *madreiga* than he. He feels so bad for not having done more honorable deeds during his lifetime. In a cemetery, we are not permitted to wear our *tzitzis* (fringes, a reminder of the 613 *mitzvos*) on the outside of our pants because we do not want to embarrass the deceased who cannot perform any more *mitzvos*.

Shir Hashirim[44] speaks about the great love and devotion between *Klal Yisrael*[45] and *HaShem*. We see from Shir Hashirim how the love of G-d and His people extends beyond that which is humanly possible. It is a love that is at the same time simple and deeper than anything else in the world. In our interpersonal relationships, if someone tries to get too close to us, we often build a wall to keep them at an emotional distance. *HaShem* is so close that we seem to do the same to Him. We push Him away [by sinning] even though we know He wants to be close to us. The love between a husband and wife gives insight and understanding into what it means to love *HaShem*. It is greater than either individual and transcends measurement.

Reb Moshe Chaim Luzzatto says that real love and fear of *HaShem* bring a person nearer to his Creator and form a bond of attachment to Him. Just as in any relationship *bein adom l'chavero* - between man and his neighbor - one must love *HaShem* unconditionally, rather than for potential rewards or from fear of punishment.[46] When one stands in awe before *HaShem*'s greatness, he is purified of the darkness associated with his physical body and is enveloped by the Divine Presence. The purification and envelopment grow in relation to the magnitude of this awe. Moshe Rabbeinu[47] attained this perfection, as our Sages teach us, "With regard to Moshe, fear [of *HaShem*] was a small thing."[48] The Divine Presence continuously surrounded Moshe because of his constant awe of *HaShem*. We too can be enveloped in awe of *HaShem*, but many of us go through life as if asleep. We follow the commandments by rote rather than with consciousness and intent. Our *neshamos*,[49] however, are constantly attached to *HaShem Yisborach*.[50] We are constantly showered with *HaShem*'s Divine Light, which sustains us. So why do we seem to ignore this and not live in awe of our Creator as we should?

From the Torah we learn to appreciate all of creation. Torah opens the door to look inward and so effects positive change. Rabbi Eliyahu Lopian taught that if man lived like a beast without understanding, but

---

44 Song of songs
45 The Jewish people
46 Zohar 1:11b
47 Moses
48 Berachos 33b
49 Souls
50 Our Creator

could reflect on the deeds of the Creator, he would overflow with dread and trembling at the majestic splendor of *HaShem*. 'Raise your eyes on high and see; who created these?'[51] If it were possible to comprehend everything on earth and not take its very existence for granted, one would be astounded. Since we are born on earth, everything in our surroundings seems commonplace and we are unimpressed by it. For this reason, the prophet Isaiah instructed us to look at the heavens, with which we are not yet familiar, 'and see Who created these?' In any of the thousands of state and national parks, one can appreciate the hand of *HaShem*. One needs only to open one's eyes to see that we are surrounded by *HaShem's* glory in even the most mundane moments of our daily lives. We are desensitized to our surroundings and do not notice the magnificence of our world. If only we could remove the blindfolds and truly see! As easy as it is to see the beauty and experience the thrill of the waves of the ocean, so too our own lives are constantly filled with excitement.

Rebbe Nachman teaches that one should look for the natural sensibility of all that occurs in our daily lives.[52] It is important to recognize and accept that everything *HaShem* does is for good. Sometimes it is easy to pinpoint this good; at other times we have to rely on our faith and trust to believe that there is good in difficult situations that are beyond our understanding. We must assure ourselves that, at the proper time, *HaShem* will show us His reasons, even if the explanation must wait until the time of *Moshiach*[53] or when we ascend to the next world. Remember that *HaShem* loves us and does what is best. When this thought process is internalized to the best of our ability, fear of Heaven and joy will come easily. There is, after all, so much for which to be thankful and joyous.

When one serves *HaShem* every moment, there is no room for arrogance, foolish pride or other negative character traits.[54] It is vital to make one's entire being a *k'li*[55] in which the *Shechinah* can rest. "Your thought should always be secluded with the *Shechinah*, thinking only of your continuous love for Her that She may be attached to you." Say constantly in your mind, 'When will I merit that the light of the *Shechinah* abides with me?'[56]

Rashi explains, "In all my deeds, I have placed His fear before my eyes. Why? Because He is always at my right hand to help me so that I should not falter." Our scholars of times past were devoted to the practice of *shivisi HaShem l'negdi samid*. The Rachmei ha-Av teaches, "You should

---

51 Isaiah 40:26
52 Likutey Maharan 1
53 Messiah
54 Tzava'at Harivash 52
55 Vessel
56 Tzava'at Harivash 8

have continuous *deveikus* - connection - with *HaShem*, blessed be He, and you should not lose it for even one minute. One should become accustomed, immediately upon awakening, to say continually, 'Blessed is the One and Only One,' and the verse, 'I have placed the *HaShem* before me always, or at least the word *shivisi*, I have placed."[57] Rabbi Yaakov Koppel Chassid, a disciple of the Baal Shem Tov, would constantly verbalize throughout the day, "I have placed *HaShem* before me always," even during work and business.[58] In the name of the Arizal, of blessed memory, it has been written that one should always picture the Divine Name *YKVK* before his eyes.[59] This is the hidden meaning of the verse, 'I have placed *HaShem* before me always," and it is of considerable benefit in attaining fear of Heaven.'[60]

Once, while riding on the highway, Rabbi Avigdor Miller shouted to the driver to stop. Thinking a tire had blown, the driver pulled to the side of the road immediately. The Rabbi got out of the car and stood towards the corner of the road. Realizing that there were no problems with the car, the driver patiently waited, and upon his passenger's return, the bewildered driver asked what was wrong. Rabbi Miller responded, 'I forgot about *HaShem* for a brief moment.'

The pious Rabbi Yitzchok of Drobitch traveled from town to town giving over Torah. One ice-cold winter he was traveling on the road by foot when some fellow Jews passed in a carriage and, having compassion, took him into the carriage. During the journey, they came upon a river. Without warning, Rabbi Yitzchok leaped off the carriage, removed his garments and jumped into the frozen river. The others looked on in astonishment. After a few minutes, Rabbi Yitzchok emerged, dressed and returned to the carriage. His fellow travelers asked Rabbi Yitzchok to explain his actions. He answered, 'My practice is to always have the name YKVK before my eyes, in black fire on a background of white fire. While we were traveling, at that moment, it disappeared from before me. So, I went into the river and pleaded, 'Master of the World, if you return to me, good; but if not, why should I live any longer?' And it was returned to me.'[61]

Rabbi Isaac ben Solomon of Acco once remarked, "I proclaim this both to individuals and the masses who wish to know the mystery of binding one's soul on high. One can attach his thoughts to *HaShem* and, when one does so consistently, there is no question that he will be worthy

---

57 Rachmei Ha-Av #16 Deveikus
58 Tiferet Beit David pg.103
59 Before attempting to write *HaShem*'s name, one must learn the appropriate laws, including not causing disgrace by erasing the Name. It is forbidden to think Torah thoughts in a rest room, place of filth or in the midst of immodesty.
60 First Simon in Mishnah Berurah
61 Missions Chassidim- pg.415, #7

of the world to come, and *HaShem*'s name will be with him constantly, both in this world and the next. You should constantly keep the letters of the Unique Name in your mind as if they were in front of you, written in a book with Torah *ashuris* script. Each letter should appear infinitely large. When you depict the letters of the Unique Name in this manner, your mind's eye should gaze on them, and at the same time, your heart should be directed toward the *Ain Sof* [62]. Your gazing and thought should be as one. This is the mystery of true attachment, regarding which the Torah says, "To Him, you shall attach yourself." [63] If you are able to do this, no evil will befall you. You will not be subject to errors caused by logic or emotion, and you will not be the victim of accidents. If you are attached to *HaShem*, you are above all accidents, and are in control of events." [64]

Dovid HaMelech was constantly attached to *HaShem*. When it came time to leave this world, *Satan* had to trick Dovid to distract from his Torah learning by shaking the trees. At that moment, the Angel of Death was able to snatch King Dovid's soul. [65]

"The Torah of *YKVK* is complete." [66] All the words of the Torah are woven and connected from this name of *HaShem*. [67] "*YKVK, Elokim* formed man out of the dust of the ground, and breathed into his nostrils a soul-breath, *neshama*, of life; man thus became a living creature." [68] Why are we supposed to meditate on this particular name of *HaShem* and not another? This name is the cause of all causes and the source of all sources. Included in it are all things, from *Keter* [69] to the lowliest gnat. It is forbidden to pronounce this name in any form whatsoever. Instead, during our *tefillos*, [70] we say the *Cognomen Adna*. [71] *YKVK* is the holiest of *HaShem*'s names, through which a person can climb to the highest spiritual levels.

The word *shivisi* derives from the root-word *shaveh*, which means equal. *Histavus* - equanimity - is a fundamental principle in attaining piety. Rabbi Moshe, a disciple of Rabbi Joseph Gikatalia, once said, "If a person's heart impels him to rectify his traits, perfecting his personality and deeds, he should pursue humility to the ultimate degree. He should be insulted but not insult, hear himself scorned but not respond. The Divine Presence will then immediately rest on him and he will not have to learn from any mortal

---

62 Unique Being
63 Deuteronomy 10:20
64 Meir Eynayim, Ekev
65 *Shabbos* 30
66 Psalms 19:8
67 Sha'are Orah, intro
68 Genesis 2:7
69 Literally crown, Keter is the highest Sefirah - spiritual realm
70 Prayers
71 Word replacing the name of *HaShem*, YKVK. Adon-ay means our Master; unless we are praying, we do not say this Name in vain.

being, for the spirit of *HaShem* will teach him."[72] The Baal Shem Tov explains *histavus* as follows: "No matter what happens, whether people praise or shame you, as with anything else, it is all the same to you. This applies likewise to any food; it is all the same to you whether you eat delicacies or other things. The *Yetzer Hara* is entirely removed from you. Whatever happens, you should say, 'It comes from *HaShem*, blessed be He, and if it is proper in His eyes...' Your motives are for the sake of Heaven; for yourself, nothing makes any difference. To accept such equanimity, one must reach a very high *madreiga*. You must serve *HaShem* with all of your might because everything is 'required [for the above].' You must attach yourself to *HaShem* and effect *yichudim* - unifications. If you are on a trip, unable to pray and study, as usual, you must serve *HaShem* in other ways. *HaShem* wishes to be served in all possible ways. Opportunities and obstacles occur every day to afford us the ability to serve Him in an alternate manner."[73]

Wherever you are, you must be careful not to sin. An 'average' person will do holy things everywhere, such as pray, say a blessing over food, etc. Each man is destined from on high to be in a particular place at a given time. At that time and place, there is something that he must correct.[74] If, Heaven forbid, your tire blows on the road there is a purpose for it. Perhaps you are meant to meet the person who will stop to help you, allowing that person to do a *mitzvah*. Maybe you must stay in that town for *Shabbos* and your host will perform the *mitzvah* of *hachnoses orchim*.[75] Rather than becoming depressed because of an unplanned stop, try to be joyous and happy that *HaShem* leads you on the pathways He knows is best.

"Fortunate is he whose transgression is borne, whose sin is covered."[76] A person goes to a friend or psychologist to unburden his emotions, so we must do the same with our sins by regular confession. When we haven't confessed our sins before *HaShem*, these sins become barriers that prevent our drawing close to Him. Sins we have not confessed are brought by angels before HaShem for judgment.

Rebbe Nachman teaches that, when a person is judged with the judgment of Heaven, justice becomes clothed in all things and all things become *HaShem*'s messengers for carrying out "The written judgment."[77] When a person judges himself there is no judgment from Above; fear does not clothe itself in anything to arouse the person because he has aroused himself. When a person achieves true *yiras HaShem*[78] through self-judgment,

---

72 Reishis Chachmah, Anavah 3
73 Tzava'at Harivash 2-3
74 Sichos Haran 85
75 Welcoming guests
76 Psalms 31:1
77 Psalms 149:9

it will lead to *daas*.[79] When a person has *daas*, he merits increased perception of the Torah. The Torah dwells with a person who has this *daas*, but he must also have fear in order to have *daas*. "*HaShem* gives wisdom (Torah) to the wise (a wise person is someone with *daas*)."[80] We should not allow one evening to pass without self-reflection and confession to *HaShem*.[81]

A person should always place his sins before him. When he was about eighty years old Rabbi Eliyahu Lopian remarked, "I can remember in detail every one of my deeds since I was twelve years old up to the present moment."[82]

Rabbi Tzadok ha-Cohen of Lublin said, "The real meaning of the entire Torah is the remembrance of *HaShem*; the rest is just numerous counsels, for every time and place and situation, how to come to that remembrance. The intention in all of them is that your awareness of *HaShem's* Presence shall not depart for a minute and that forgetfulness will not conquer you, Heaven forbid."[83]

Rabbeinu Yonah writes, "Of those men who do not arrange their thoughts, to reflect regularly on the fear of *HaShem*, it is said: 'Their fear of Me is a commandment of men learned by rote.'"[84] Let us not be among those who go about their everyday life without putting aside time to reflect upon the fear of Heaven. Isaiah[85] says, "When the holy *Moshiach* comes, all the nations will fear *HaShem*.[86] On that day YKVK will be One and His Name One."[87] "The end of the matter, all having been heard: Fear *HaShem* and keep his *mitzvos*, for this is the whole of man."[88]

We have already seen from Proverbs, "The beginning of wisdom is the fear of *HaShem*." Therefore, the key to *Avodas HaShem* is to constantly recognize before Whom you stand, the Holy One blessed be He. Rabbi Chanina ben Dosa said, "Whenever a person's fear of sin comes before his wisdom, his wisdom will endure; but when a person's wisdom comes before his fear of sin, his wisdom will not endure."[89]

Having true fear of *HaShem* is a job you have to work on your entire life. It isn't something that can be accomplished overnight but, as you have learned here, there are many methods of coming closer to *HaShem* and

---

78 Fear of Heaven
79 Understanding
80 Daniel 2:21
81 Likutey Maharan 15
82 Lev Eliyahu p.xx
83 Tzidkas ha-Tzaddik, #232
84 Shaarei Teshuvah 3:15
85 Our Sages
86 Isaiah 43:5-6
87 Zechariah 14:9
88 Koheles 12:13
89 Pirkei Avos 3:11

increasing your fear of Him. The most important thing to remember is that "In all your ways acknowledge Him and He will direct your path."[90] Never forget that you stand before Him always and place the thought of Him in your mind as you go through life, *"Shivisi HaShem lenegdi samid* - I have placed the L-rd before me constantly."[91]

---

90 Proverbs 3:6
91 Psalms 16:8

TEFILAH FOR AVODAS HASHEM

HaShem, thank you so much for giving me the opportunity to serve You with love and to fear Your name. I am taught that fear of Heaven is the beginning of wisdom but, HaShem, I am so far from real fear. The great tzaddikim would tremble as they said Your Holy Name in prayer, while I run through it as if it were just another word. Not only do I lack sufficient awe of Your Name, but I also fail to serve You out of love. At times, I do so by rote and fear alone. My expectations for myself are higher than this; nonetheless, I continue to repeat the error of my ways. I turn to You, HaShem, for help, asking, begging to experience the true meaning of Yiras HaShem and love for You.

I want to engrave the passuk from Dovid HaMelech, 'Shivisi HaShem Linegdi Samid', in my mind and heart. HaShem, You know how difficult it is for me to practice this as my mind constantly wanders from place to place. Only You, HaShem, can help me to make this great teaching a reality. Help me, HaShem, not to sleep away the days of my life. Assist me in making my heart and service of You authentic. I need Your help and the inner strength to follow all the laws of the Shulchan Aruch. I know how important it is to follow all the laws, but sometimes I become overwhelmed just trying to keep my life in order. My Yetzer Hara can be so strong and convincing that at times I do foolish things. I even shock myself to think, HaShem, that while I am making my grievous mistakes, Your sustenance remains my lifeline. I don't understand why You keep providing me with more opportunities when I have failed miserably at the ones You've already given me. Your mercy, love, and patience with me are beyond the comprehension of the angels, let alone someone of earthly form.

If only I feared and loved You as I know I should, I would be a much greater person than I am today. When will I merit that the light of the Shechinah abides with me? At what point in my life will I finally realize that there is nothing more important than to serve You with love and fear? HaShem, please help me to never forget from where I came and before Whom I stand, bowed in gratitude. Help me to avoid a heart full of pride, thinking I'm above my neighbor in honorable deeds. Let me not go through life making excuses for events that surround me; let me realize Your hand in everything and not attribute it to 'luck' or 'the regular course of nature'. Help me to recognize Your Hand in my life, protecting me from evil and mishap. Let me not leave this world without repenting for my sins. Please help me to follow the advice of the great sages, to make an accounting of my actions every evening.

HaShem, it is so important to acquire fear of Heaven. A person can't become a tzaddik and grow in his Yiddishkeit without proper fear of You. I could serve You without love, but Your glory would never reach into the deepest recesses of my heart. Rebbono Shel Olam, You have given us so many reasons to be thankful. Of the thousands of things, You do for us each day, we cannot recognize even a fraction. Please know that we are sincerely grateful.

CHAPTER 2: SIMCHA, JOY

"Be wise, my son, and my heart will gladden". (Proverbs 27:11)

Many of us try to attain great levels of purity and *avodas HaShem* but find our labors to be unfruitful. This may be because we lack a certain principal ingredient in our view of life. This ingredient is joy. Without happiness in one's heart, great devotions will not rise to the heights. We will serve *HaShem* but not be able to handle the ups and downs in our religious devotions. We can still attain a lot from our love for *mitzvos* but won't serve *HaShem* with full potential.

Doctors call ours the Prozac generation: People have never struggled so much to find relief from emotional distress. "A happy heart is as healing as medicine."[92] The only way to have a truly happy heart is to "Cast your burden on *HaShem*, and He will sustain you."[93] Many of us keep our emotions bottled up until we're ready to burst. Rather, we should tell *HaShem* our troubles and not live a life of sorrow. As hard as it might be, we should find a person to whom we can unburden our heart. This helps put our troubles in perspective and we might see that they aren't as bad as we thought. They might seem almost trivial once we verbalize and share them.

Sometimes we find it hard to think positive thoughts, but in fact, there is so much to be thankful for. Rabbi Avigdor Miller says, "A person who is depressed has a lack of *hakaros hatov* [94] for what he has been given." We could make a list of everything we're grateful for and read it every morning. If we find our mind dwelling on negative thoughts during the day, we can read the list again. Do we thank *HaShem* for the simple things? When we walk the hallways of a hospital or nursing home, it is virtually impossible to ignore the things we take for granted. Seeing someone on a

---

92 Mishlei 17:22
93 Tehillim 55:23
94 Appreciation

respirator helps us value our ability to breathe. Seeing someone in a wheelchair being fed, having lost the use of his arms and legs, helps us value the ability to eat and walk. Such sights remind us to take care of our bodies, appreciate the gift of life, and not squander our lives on depression for things we can't change. Must we lose the important things we've been given in order to appreciate and be thankful for them? Do we ever thank *HaShem* for the window wipers in our car or the belt loops in our pants?

In our busy and confusing lives, we are often faced with the need to find joy. Not knowing what else to do, we reach for some object that we think will make us happy. If we believe the media, the road to happiness is paved with diamonds, new luxury cars, electronic equipment and extravagant vacations. Unfortunately, many people seek these material answers only to find that, after getting what they yearned for, they are still unhappy. To make matters worse, not only have these people yet to find their happiness but now they are also deeply in debt, paying for the tangible representation of an intangible goal. *Chazal* teach that a person dies with only half of the materialistic possessions he wanted. The more money he has, the more he craves. One who sets his sights on earning a specific amount of money, and acquires that amount, never stops. The goal becomes to earn as much as possible.

How is a child supposed to grow up self-sufficient and happy with what he can afford if we give him everything he desires and more, spoiling him for eighteen or twenty years? If our children see us desperately craving the latest gadgets, how will they learn to be content without the newest toys? Can anyone find happiness within him-or-herself?

If we were stuck on a desert island, could our family members enjoy each other's company? Let us learn to be happy with life itself. We must show those we love that we appreciate spending time with them, even if there is nothing to do together or talk about. We don't need box seats for a ball game to spend time with our loved ones. In fact, we need nothing but each other. When our children are grown, will they recall the time we bought another toy, or will they remember the special times spent together as a family? For every thirty matchbox cars or dolls, will your future teenager need thirty different types of shoes? Will our children know how to be happy with their lot if the example they see is sadness and craving?

Our grandparents used to appreciate their families and the simple portion given to them. We, on the other hand, are never satisfied with one another or our possessions. Instead of love for our neighbor, today we think, let us love ourselves and then our neighbor or spouse. My grandfather, Yaakov ben Shlomo Zavel *z"l* didn't have any trouble being humble; it was a given to him.

HaShem accepts and loves us regardless of the car we drive, where we live or what we do for *parnosa* (livelihood). We need to incorporate that love, so we can believe in Him. Our lack of joy can stem from a lack of *emunah* in *HaShem*. Rebbe Nachman teaches that talking about trust in *HaShem* helps one increase his *emunah*. Even when our initial goal is to help someone else increase his *emunah*, it will also help increase our own. When we trust in *HaShem* we have no alternative but to be happy.

We need self-love, but not to the exclusion of others. The basis of Torah, 'Love your neighbor as yourself', clearly instructs us to love others, but we can only do so when we first love ourselves.

In our overloaded schedules, time should be reserved for enjoyment. There will always be something to worry about: family, children, health, house, car, finances, and work. If we fret over these things, we may never have a moment's peace and will, *chas v'sholom,*[95] end up physically or emotionally ill. Medical science has identified the people most likely to endure serious illness, based on a set of character traits. People with a Type A personality are more likely to suffer heart attacks, strokes, and gastrointestinal disorders. They rarely stop agonizing over things long enough to relax and enjoy life. We transmit this stress to our children by overloading their schedules as well. Scout or youth groups used to be the only after-school recreation activity for children; today their calendars resemble busy executives. There are music and foreign language lessons, sports, and tutoring - not for remediation but to compete and excel. Our children are getting the message at a very young age that it's not enough to go to school, come home and do homework. Psychologists agree that children today are growing up with too much pressure from all these activities. They have little time to enjoy being children, due to their parents' lack of satisfaction with some aspect of their own lives.

All of us go through ups and downs emotionally and physically. We search and search for the answer to all of our problems but we many times just end up going around in circles. The only way to truly search for answers is through a joyous heart. It is written, "You shall emerge with joy."[96] Through joy, you can emerge from all troubles.[97]

A question we sometimes face is where to find joy in our busy and sometimes confusing life. Not knowing what else to do, we reach for materialistic answers - only to find them to be shooting after the wind. The Torah is a splendid light and brings joy to one's heart, yet we continue to reach for empty shadows. The thought, "I am depressed; I must learn more Torah," doesn't seem to come up often enough in our evaluations.

There is a *passuk* in Devarim, which says, "Because you did not serve *HaShem* with happiness…"[98] The Kotzker Rebbe explains this as

---

95 G-D forbid
96 Isaiah 55:12
97 Rabbi Menachem Mendel of Kotzk
98 Devarim 28:47

follows: "Our nation was warned here that if they do not listen to *HaShem* and follow in His ways, they will provoke severe chastisement. They will be punished specifically because they "Did not serve… with happiness." If a person does not serve *HaShem* with happiness, does that warrant this stern rebuke? The meaning of the verse is that not only did you not serve *HaShem*, but also you were happier that you did not serve Him![99]

"G-d chastises those He loves".[100] How can we explain why suffering is a sign of G-d's love? Think about parenting. Why do we set limits and punish our children when they don't obey the rules we have set for them? We love our children and want them to grow to be responsible, kind, generous adults. If they don't learn when they are young, they won't know the proper way to act when we are no longer standing over, coaching their every move. The same is true of *HaShem*. He gives us rules - the Torah and *mitzvos* – which we are expected to follow. No one is totally free of sins; even the greatest *tzaddik* has a few sins for which he must do *teshuva*. For us to go on to *Olam Habah* - the World to Come - free of spiritual blemishes, we must be cleansed of our sins in this world.

There are people who seemingly have no cares in the world. They go through life smiling, singing and spreading cheer to those around them. It's surprising to find that some of these people lead very difficult lives. Reb Zusia lived in poverty and constant pain. One day, a stranger passing through asked the village rabbi to explain how one could be expected to thank *HaShem* when terrible things happen. The rabbi told him to ask Reb Zusia. The stranger found Reb Zusia in a tiny hut with only the dirt for a floor. There was little furniture, no heat and scarcely any food to feed the large family. When the stranger asked his question, Reb Zusia replied 'I don't know why the rabbi thought I could help you. I've never experienced anything bad in my life.' The traveler left, understanding the rabbi's lesson.

Almost everyone has good days and bad days. Our individual paths are full of curves and blind spots. When the road is flat and straight, you don't have to search to find happiness; it is there. When a fog permeates the air, as on a bad day, you keep searching but your heart comes up with nothing. There are times when visibility drops so much that you think to yourself, 'How will I get through the next hour?' We must cultivate *emunah* - faith.

When everything goes well, we think it's because we did something right and forget to thank *HaShem*. If we are born into wealth, we think that everything comes our way because of our parents and we do not learn to depend on *HaShem*. Does a child who grows up with servants tending to his every need learn to be self-sufficient? To draw close to *HaShem*, we need strength of character.

---

99 And Nothing but the Truth p. 18
100 Proverbs 3:12

Rebbe Nachman says, "The entire world is a narrow bridge; the main thing is not to fear." During grim times, separate yourself from your present slump and focus on your good points. View yourself in a positive light. Remembering your good points during emotionally trying times should be a frequent practice in your *avodas HaShem*.

Rabbi Menachem Schneerson taught an eye-opening reality: "Much depression comes from haughtiness. If you would realize who you really are, you wouldn't be so disappointed with yourself."[101] Rabbi Schneerson goes on to explain, "Depression is not a crime, but it lowers a person into an abyss deeper than any crime could reach. Depression is a scheme instigated by the self-destructive elements within all of us. Once depressed, a person can easily make mistakes.

Rabbi Nosson once remarked that the evil inclination cares less about the sin than the depression that follows, since by that means it can further trap the person and gain many more sins than the first. If we make the mistake of transgressing, we should feel remorse but not allow ourselves to feel depression. It is vital to fight depression as one would his greatest enemy; run from it as he would from death itself.[102]

The Baal Shem Tov said, "The main rule in serving *HaShem* is that you should keep yourself from sadness to the very best of your ability."[103] "Without joy, it is impossible to be attached constantly to *HaShem*."[104]

When you observe a commandment with joy, this is a sign that your heart is complete with *HaShem*.[105] Nothing is more pleasant in the world than a *mitzvah* completed with joy. It is like entering a whole other world. How pleasant and rewarding it is to take but a moment and reflect upon the joy of the *mitzvah*. "You should feel so happy when you do a *mitzvah* that you do not do it just to receive a reward in the future world. You want *HaShem* to send you another *mitzvah*, this being the reward for the first one. This is because your joy is in the *mitzvah*.[106] "The joy of the *mitzvos* is the perfection of holiness."[107]

Rebbe Nachman teaches that thinking about the precious gifts we are given, simply by being Jewish, brings us happiness. We have been given the gift of *Olam Habah* - the World to Come - and the opportunity to perform 613 *mitzvos* to draw us close to *HaShem*. Rebbe Nachman says that overcoming sadness is one of the hardest tasks given to man. The only way to overcome it can sometimes be through foolish ways. One must and can

101 Bringing Heaven Down to Earth #120
102 Ibid. #114
103 Likutey Yekarim 1b
104 Ibid, 2b
105 Sefer Hamidos, simcha
106 Likutey Etzos, simcha #2
107 Likutey Etzos, simcha #9

rise above it. There is no life in a depressed world. We must place our thoughts in a world of happiness. The Seer of Lublin, in the name of the Arizal, said, "When a person is sunk in a depressive state, no advice can help him. He must simply wait until the anger passes... When the moment of happiness suddenly arrives, all of his problems will then be solved."[108] We must place our thoughts in a world of happiness. Rebbe Levi Yitzchok of Berditchev would always recite the *birchas hashachar* (morning prayers) aloud with the congregation. As he was leading the prayers one morning, he passed over the blessing *shelo asani goy*, which praises *HaShem* 'for not making me a gentile.' After the prayers, a few congregants asked him the reason for this omission. "Upon awakening this morning," The *rebbe* replied, "I was overcome with intense joy at having been born a Jew. I could therefore not contain myself and felt obliged to recite this blessing without any hesitation."[109]

Every time a person thinks of something joyous, *Satan* counters it with sadness. The only thought *Satan* cannot degrade is that we are Jews, not heathens. This is our greatest joy, and it can't be confounded by outside forces. The Jewish heart and soul are special. When you feel as if all hope is lost, the way to rise above it is to think how lucky you are to be a Jew. Being Jewish is so powerful that you can't ever lose your identity. A Jewish soul lives forever, in this world and the next. Our charitable deeds carry on for eternity and not a single good deed is lost. For this reason, we have a great responsibility to the world. Every one of us can make a difference just because of our Jewish *neshama* - soul. We have an obligation to find that special treasure within ourselves and share it with others.

The Torah is a splendid light and brings joy to one's heart, yet we rarely recognize its value to our lives. We may think that observing all the *mitzvos* is too hard, especially when we are depressed. If we recognize that all our strength comes from *HaShem*, we will see that nothing He expects of us is beyond our ability. The Torah provides spiritual strength for those who seek it. If you normally exercise every day, you know how energized you feel. If you miss even one day, it is difficult to complete your regular exercise routine the next day and you may be tempted to skip another day. When you return to exercise after missing a few days, you have to struggle to keep up with your normal pace. The same is true of Torah. If you ignore it for one day, it ignores you longer. When adversity comes, people frequently lament 'Why me? I can't take it anymore!' But *HaShem* knows exactly how much we 'can take' and never gives more than we can handle. It's often difficult to find something positive in troublesome situations, but we must remember that what seems negative now may well turn out to be positive.

---

108 Zichron Zos
109 From my Father's *Shabbos* Table p.79

Everyone likes to give and receive gifts, but sometimes we worry that the gift we've chosen will not be the right size or color. Still, we know that simply receiving the gift will elevate the spirits of both giver and receiver. There is a gift that anyone can give, regardless of financial situation, and the best news is that one size fits all. We can give the gift of a smile and a joyous greeting. It costs nothing to put on a happy face. Try this experiment when you are walking in a crowded area: Nod your head and smile at each person you see. Smiling and happiness are contagious: It keeps on passing from one person to the next, and soon everyone is smiling. There is bound to be at least one person who is having a difficult day but, when he receives the smile, his troubles will be lifted, even if for a moment. When enough people smile and greet that person, he won't be able to hold onto his troubling thoughts; the collective unit of people will have helped raise his spirits. If each of us practiced smiling, what a happy world it would be! Even if we fake an outward smile, it's bound to have a positive effect on us. Rabbeinu Bachya teaches: "The pious person carries his pain within, while his face radiates joy." Rebbe Nachman says, "If you have to, force yourself to be happy and soon after it will become a reality for you."[110] Rabbi Dr. Abraham Twerski, the noted psychiatrist, says that smiling, even when alone, leads to a positive outlook.

Our sages tell us that each of us forms part of a limb of the original man, Adam haRishon. Each of us contains an important ingredient that the world needs us to share with others. Some of us have found our unique calling, while others are still in the searching process. Being a Jew is so powerful that one cannot convert to another religion and lose his status as a Jew. A Jew is forever, in two worlds. We have a great responsibility to the world. We have been placed on the front lines of *HaShem*'s army. Every one of us can make a difference just because of our Jewish *neshama*, soul. It is a thrill to share this uniqueness with one another.

HaShem has blessed us with the ability to keep *Shabbos* with an extra *neshama* shining into us. The joy in observing the festivals of *Chanukah*, *Pesach*, *Sukkos*, *Purim*, *Shavuos* and *Rosh Hashanah* can be out of this world. We have all been born with a silver spoon of joy in our hands; may we only be able to recognize and appreciate this.

The Midrash teaches us that *HaShem* gave *Adam* and *Chava* (Eve) a blessing as they were about to leave the Garden of Eden. He said, "I give you the gift of forgetfulness." *Simcha* – joy - spelled in Hebrew hints at the verse, "And *HaShem* will wipe away tears from all faces" (Isaiah 25:8).[111] What is the secret for attaining joy? If you recall every hurt ever done to you, you will never be able to smile. If we never forgive others for hurting us, we will always have enmity in our hearts. Even if we mend the

---

110 Until the Moshiach, p. 334
111 The Secrets of Hebrew Words

relationship, if we have a slight animosity toward another person, we hurt ourselves as well. No one can be happy if he harbors resentments. Once we forgive we must let go of anger, even towards ourselves. Forgetting is easy; it happens whether or not we desire it. Forgiveness takes conscious effort but is vital to our happiness.

The world seems to always be going either too fast or too slow. There does not seem to be time to enjoy anything. Either we are worrying about our finances and possessions, or we are stressed over common situations. This world is a confusing place. That is the way it's supposed to be when we live without the *emes*[112] of the future days of *Moshiach*. As frustrating as our life seems to be, we must go with the flow, so to speak, and be happy even through the hardest trials.

The Vilna Gaon once stated that all our actions in this world, whether physical or spiritual, are comparable to planting a seed. All we can do is plow and sow, whereas the rain and dew, blight and rot, are completely up to *HaShem*. A person must toil but not waste time worrying about the results, which remain in *HaShem's* hands. If a Jew spends his entire day in Torah study, he should be happy to be doing what *HaShem* asks of him. Each day he should move forward, without worrying about yesterday's results. He must also beg *HaShem* for success, but the desire for progress should not blind him to his gradual, daily growth. Fruits that ripen after a long time, having overcome many obstacles and trials, are sweeter than those that come sooner.[113]

If you look at the great *tzaddikim* of our generation, you will see that many have a humorous side. To take on such a significant role in *Klal Yisrael* and carry so much weight on their shoulders, they must sometimes joke around a little bit. I once met a great rabbi who translates some of the most difficult Torah passages into English. Before meeting him, I pictured him with a serious nature; instead, I encountered a very happy, down-to-earth man.

Rabbi Chayim Zaitchyk said, "Be aware of the great value in being alive. When you realize the great treasure that lies in every second of life, you will experience the great joy in each moment. This awareness will motivate you to utilize each moment to its fullest."[114]

Nobody wants someone who is depressed to be close to him. Someone once asked the Nikolsburger Rebbe why he didn't have so many friends. He answered, "People don't want to be around someone who is sad." We have to work on our happiness, and then we can enter the palace of the King and people will enjoy our company.

A person can do a lot of good deeds all his life, but if it is without

---

112 Truth
113 In All Your Ways P.38
114 Consulting The Wise, Zelig Pliskin

simchas hachayim, the joy of life, what meaning does it have? *HaShem* does not want us to go through life sad. I have met people whose hearts were so broken and full of sadness I do not know how they managed. This is not for us. There is no life in a world of sadness. There is no reason why one cannot pull himself out of this pit of depression and live in a joyous world.

Rebbe Nachman says that the way to release oneself from illness is to be joyous. Depression sinks a person even deeper into his illness. Happiness is an important cure for illness because, when a person is happy, he is able to make true reflections about himself and his life. This brings a person to complete *teshuvah.*

When a person becomes ill, his legs feel heavy. Usually, when you feel depressed or sick you can feel this heaviness. This is because the right and left legs of man correspond to the *sefiros,* Netzach and *Hod,* in the spiritual realms. The judgment for a person's sins corresponds to these *sefiros.* If you are sick and down, Rebbe Nachman says to get up and dance, thereby elevating these Divine judgments back to their source, *Binah,* which corresponds to one's heart. By lifting one's legs into the air, one is elevating divine judgment back up to *Binah* through a heart full of joy.

When feeling down, it's good to dance because "Through dancing and body motion, joy is aroused."[115] There doesn't have to be anyone around when you dance. Jump around and clap your hands. You don't even have to be good at it to enjoy dancing; it's a universal happiness. If you don't know what to do and are confused, just start dancing. I was once faced with tremendous confusion and pain. In the distance I spotted a parking lot, so I walked there and just started dancing. The Holy Baal Shem Tov used to dance to increase his religious *hislahavus,* enthusiasm, and *d'vekus.* He taught his followers that "The dances of the Jew before his Creator are prayers," as it says in Psalms, "All my bones shall say *HaShem,* who is like unto Thee?"[116]

Every *Shabbos* night a crowd would surround Rabbi Moshe Leib of Sassov in order to watch him dance in honor of the *Shabbos* queen. His dancing was one of thirsting and yearning to draw close to *HaShem.* The entire house was filled with the light of *kedusha*[117], as even the angels came and danced with him (though not seen by those observing this event). For hours he would dance on and on, utterly divorced from materiality, without tiring.[118]

It says in Talmud Arachin 11a, "Which is the service of joy and happiness? It is song." The essence of *devekus,* attachment to *HaShem,* is through the melody.[119] Musical instruments and melody have a great power

---

115 Sefer Hamidos, simcha #8
116 Psalm 35:10 (Encyclopedia Judaica, Dance, vol 5, p.1267)
117 Holiness
118 Tiferes Banim Avotam, p. 177

to draw a person closer to *HaShem*. Therefore, it is good to accustom yourself to liven up your attitude frequently with some melody. This will bring you to joy and through this, you will cleave to *HaShem*. *Shabbos* and holidays are especially good times to do this.[120]

HaShem would love nothing more than for us to serve him with simple joy and love of life. Rabbi Yehudah HaChasid taught, "The root of all prayer is a joyous heart before *HaShem*. "Glory in His holy name, rejoice you hearts that seek *HaShem*."[121] King David accompanied all his prayers and Psalms with the harp, filling his heart with joy and love of *HaShem*.[122] A person should create ladders by which he can ascend to Heaven. A *niggun* (melody) is one such ladder, especially when you sing after experiencing the joy of a *mitzvah*.[123] A cantor or singer is called a *chazzan*, from the word *chazzon* meaning vision and prophecy, since music is derived from the same place as prophecy.[124] An expression of fervent love is to sing songs of love, as we should before *HaShem*.[125] "Which is the service of joy and happiness? It is song."[126] The essence of *devekus* is through the melody.[127] Melody has the power to draw a person closer to *HaShem*. Especially on *Shabbos* and holidays, it helps to enliven the day with a melody and connect with *HaShem*.[128]

Rabbi Meir of Premishlan lived at the bottom of a steep hill. Each day, even in the winter snow and ice, he would hike over the hill to immerse and purify his body in a stream on the other side. The people considered his actions quite wonderful since others would walk around the steep icy hill so as not to fall. No one dared to attempt the difficult climb until a few young men decided to put an end to this superstition. They boldly followed the rabbi as he effortlessly ascended the hill. The young men fell and were badly hurt. What was Rabbi Meir's secret? "When you are connected above," he explained, "you don't fall down."[129]

Our lack of joy can sometimes stem from a lack of *emunah*, trust in *HaShem*. Rebbe Nachman teaches that talking about *emunah* helps one to increase his emunah. Talk to your friends about the importance of trusting in *HaShem* and it will help you to make *emunah* in *HaShem* a reality for yourself. When you trust in *HaShem* you have no alternative than to

---

119 Likutey Aytzos, Neginah, #3
120 Ibid, #11
121 Chronicles 16:10
122 Sefer Chasidim 18
123 Tzav v'Zairuz, #36
124 Likutey Moharan 3
125 Sefer Charedim, Chapt. 34
126 Talmud Arachin 11a
127 Likutey Aytzos, Neginah, #3
128 Ibid, #11
129 Bringing Heaven Down to Earth #129

naturally be happy.

Each of our individual highways is full of curves and blind spots. There are times when fog permeates the early part of our day and other times when it manifests in the evening hours. Also, there are times when visibility drops so much that we must just stop and draw on *emunah*.

There are good days and bad days. On a good day, you do not even have to bother looking; happiness is just there. On a difficult day, you look and look until you can find it. It is so hard when you keep searching and your heart comes up with nothing during that day. Why, when we only want to do what's right, must we come up with nothing? How will we get through the next hour?

The way to find happiness during these times is to look for the good points in yourself, not only in the situation you are stuck in. Your next step is to search yourself and come up with the good you have done. For instance, think about all the commandments you did today, or a *mitzvah* you did a couple of years ago. You will then see what a good person you are. Make a list of all the *chesed* you have done for others. Finding one's good points during down times should be a common practice in a person's *avodas HaShem*. Keep the *mitzvos* and *halachos* that day very simply, without unnecessary *hanhagos*[130] you may have made for yourself. As for the good days, on them add a little extra. By giving 100% on those days, bad days will almost never come up.

Do not live a life of sorrow for years without finding a solution for your troubles. Maybe things are not as bad as they seem inside and all you need is to share your troubles with a kindly person. It could be that you truly aren't alone in your struggles, but others suffer a similar fate.

The *Satan* does not have to try so hard with us; we do most of the damage to our souls needlessly and do not even need his assistance. A person cannot serve *HaShem* properly when his heart is in pain. There is always help out there and we have to be brave enough to find it. Never forget, *HaShem* is always with us and there is no sin we can't completely repent for. As much as you need to unburden your heart to others, there will never be anyone as great as *HaShem* to talk too. He understands our soul more than anyone.

All the tools for joy have been given to you as spoken about in this chapter. You are never alone; the Torah contains all the advice needed to go from sadness to joy. Your good points are creating a great pillar for you to stand on. It is time to leave the sadness behind you.

---

130 Stringencies

TEFILAH FOR SIMCHA

Master of the world, I am grateful for everything you blessed me with. You sustain every creature, from a human being to a tiny fly. Never do You forget my family or me, as You continually provide for all of our needs. With everything You give me, I might sometimes forget to be thankful. Some of this stems from the sadness and depression I often slip into. I know there is no reason to be sad since You provide so well for me but being human I am far from perfect. I can't say I don't know how to be happy because truly I do. All I have to do is look at the family and friends I have, but I think about what I lack rather than have, which is more than I need.

Help me please HaShem in my emunah and bitachon. I know that my lack of emunah is the reason for much of my sadness. We are taught that the greatest joy comes from performing mitzvos, especially from the blessing for not being a heathen. As easy as it should be, I live without realizing how fortunate I am. When I perform mitzvos, I forget their meaning and importance. Please help me remember and recognize all the good that surrounds me.

Lead me to a life with the utmost joy and harmony in my heart. One way to attain joy is to dance and sing zemiros. Sometimes laziness overcomes me, and I don't want to exert myself. Other times I feel embarrassed that my family or friends might see me dancing and make fun of me. This is not a valid excuse since it would bring joy not only to me but also to others. Please help me to dance and sing with joy and may all my sadness turn to joy. Let the judgments against Klal Yisrael and me be full of mercy and not strict din, judgment. So many sins weigh heavily on my shoulders; please lighten the weight and help me make a new beginning in my avodas HaShem.

CHAPTER 3: OVERCOMING YOUR YETZER HARA

I [HaShem] created the evil inclination and I created the Torah as its antidote." (Baba Basra 16a)

Once, when Rabbi Pinchas of Korets entered his *beis midrash*,[131] he noticed that his students stopped conversing and then started again. He asked them what they were talking about. They responded they were saying how afraid they were that the *Yetzer Hara*[132] would pursue them. The *rebbe* responded, "Don't worry. You aren't on such a high level. You're still pursuing him!"

When I first heard this story, it really hit home for me. Every time I told it over, it shocked the listeners. It's funny how the simple words of Rabbi Pinchas of Korets contain, for most, the antidote to their struggles with the *Yetzer Hara.*

The *Yetzer Hara*, guided by *Satan*, is said to get stronger every day as a person grows in his level of *Yiddishkeit*[133]. Someone once said to his *rebbe*, "I wish I had your *Yetzer Hara*." The Rabbi, taken aback, said strongly in a stern voice, "*Chas v'Shalom*[134]." The student innocently thought that because his rabbi was so pure it must be that his *Yetzer Hara* wasn't so strong. The truth is that the higher one's level of piety, the stronger his *Yetzer Hara* has to become. After all, aren't we supposed to struggle in life with free choice? Without a *Yetzer Hara*, being pious would be easy and of little value to *HaShem* and us. To value something we must work for it and take precautions against falling into the evil inclination's trap.

Rabbi Menachem Mendel, of Kotzk, was walking down the street with his friend Reb Yitzchak, of Vorki, when they encountered an old

---

131 Study hall
132 Evil inclination
133 Judaism
134 G-D forbid

woman peddling knives. Reb Yitzchak wanted to purchase a small knife, for which the woman wanted four coins. Wanting to save some extra money, he offered her three coins. His friend, Rabbi Menachem Mendel, called him by his nickname, "Itshe! The Mishna teaches us: 'Do not converse excessively with a woman.' Now isn't that worth one copper coin?" This is an excellent example of guarding one's self so as not to fall prey to the evil inclination.

The evil urge is similar to a prankster running through a crowd, showing his tightly closed hand. No one knows what he is holding. He runs to each person and asks, "What do you suppose I have in my hand?" Each person imagines that the closed hand holds just what he desires the most. They all hurry and run after the prankster. When he has tricked them enough to follow him, the prankster opens his hand. It is empty! The same is true of the evil one. He tricks people all over the world, fooling them into following him with the thought that his hand contains what they need. In the end, the evil one opens his hand. There is nothing in it and no desire is ever fulfilled. Worldly pleasures are just like sunbeams in a dark room. They may seem solid, but when a person tries to grasp a sunbeam he finds nothing in his hand. The same is true of all worldly desires. [135]

One of the things *Satan* has us believe is that we are alone in our sin. We have sinned, and we cannot make amends. This is not true. Rebbe Nachman says, "If you believe you can damage, believe that you can fix. There is not a sin in the world that you can't repent for. The *rebbe* also says that, no matter how far you are from *HaShem* and Judaism, you can always return to the ways of the Torah. Of course, *Satan* doesn't want you to know this. Even if you do know it, he tries to give you doubts and make you lose hope for ever truly repenting.

It's interesting to note that most of us think the mistakes we make are never done by our peers. We think we're alone in our errors and view ourselves with little confidence. Even the greatest *rabbis* and *rebbetzins* have accidentally stumbled in immoral sins and then repented completely. Maybe they were stuck in these sins for years just as we are. You're never alone, my friends, and with perseverance, you will overcome the *taivos* as well! The first step, of course, is to stop repeating the sin. If you try and can't overcome it, then ask for help. For all you know, your friend or rabbi stumbled on the exact same sin and can help you out of it. Stop looking down on yourself for your sins; sometimes this is all a trick of *Satan* to make you depressed. Don't dwell on the mistakes you have made, but rather use that energy to do something about it. Repent by talking to *HaShem* and asking His forgiveness. Take a trip to a great *tzaddik* and confess your sin to him. Ask for a remedy. Confessing your sins in the

---

135 Reb Nachman's Wisdom #6

presence of a Torah scholar produces good thoughts.[136]

The sins a person commits are engraved on his very bones[137]. When he confesses them before a Torah scholar, the entire accumulation of evil engraved on his bones is lifted. All his sins are forgiven, and he is granted atonement.[138]

If you can't handle going to a living *tzaddik*, then go to the grave of a *tzaddik* and ask him to pray for you and tell him of your sin. I have met too many people in my life who kept secrets bottled up inside them for their entire lives. When they finally released their pain to someone, it gave them new life and vitality. Therefore, don't hold things in any longer.

Many people wonder why *HaShem* created evil in the world as well as good. If we didn't have an evil inclination, then we would be like robots. We would be doing the will of *HaShem* like it was nothing, without meaning or heart. It is free will that gives us the ability to be true servants of *HaShem*. Rebbe Nachman once said, "Whatever you observe in the world exists just for the sake of free will. The entire world and all its inhabitants were created only the sake of free will.[139]

I think it's the will of *HaShem* that I am blunt with you at this point. *Satan* knows that if he can get you to be depressed he will defeat you. Do whatever you can to never let this happen! Fight sadness with all your heart and limbs. Force yourself to be happy if that is what it takes.[140] If you think too much, keep yourself busy so as not to think depressing thoughts. Spend more time around family and friends who can cheer you up. Whenever I was down, I stayed away from others so as not to bring them down with me; this was an error in judgment. People are there to support one another and be a shoulder to lean on.

Every *tzaddik* is faced with the most difficult tests. *Chazal* say that the higher one's level the greater his evil inclination. There is no *tzaddik* that exists who wasn't tempted and didn't face sin head to head. We may think that because they are righteous they had never been normal human beings, facing the simple temptations we do. Yosef HaTzaddik covered his face and ran away from the most beautiful woman in the world, Potifar's wife. Rabbi Abraham Abulafia wrote that he struggled with this himself. He said, "For fifteen years, *Satan* was at my right hand to mislead me." He also said, "The numerical value of *Satan*, 359, is the same as that of Zera Lavan", white seed, a reference to semen.[141] This goes to show that one of the main goals of the *Satan* is to attack someone's sexual desire.

---

136 Sefer Hamidos 69
137 Ezekiel 32:27
138 Likutey Maharan I, 4:3
139 Tzaddik #519
140 *Rebbe* Nachman's Wisdom #20
141 Chayay Olam Habah

Rebbe Nachman says that sexual desire is the great test a man faces in this world.[142] The *rebbe* said that he was able to overcome this desire, but he had to cry out to *HaShem* again and again. The temptations were very real for him, but he later said, "A man with even the smallest amount of real intelligence will not find this a temptation at all." *Satan* wanted so much for him to slip on this desire that he was willing to let the *rebbe* overcome every other desire if only he would slip up on this once. The *rebbe* did the opposite, though, and said he would ignore his other desires and not work to control them at all but the sexual desire he would completely eradicate.[143] As a young man, even amidst the fire burning inside him, he overcame this desire completely. He later said, "I do not have any feeling of desire at all. Men and women are all the same to me." When he came in contact with a woman, he didn't even have an extraneous thought.[144]

Another time the *rebbe* said, "I am afraid of neither women nor angels." This deserves further explanation. A person may totally cleanse himself of evil thoughts. However, as long as he has the slightest fear of such thoughts, he is not completely cleansed. This slight fear is a sign that he has not yet attained complete purity. Therefore, he must fear an angel."[145]

One shouldn't fear the evil inclination; rather he should be aware and cautious of falling into its traps. When you fear anything, you cause yourself to lose control. The only one to fear is *HaShem*. Fearing the evil inclination is like giving into it.[146] Rabbi Pinchos of Koritz once said, "When a person is scared of something, he is actually subjugated to that very thing. If he is not afraid, he remains above it."[147]

King Dovid was the most devout of men, Samson was the strongest, and Solomon the wisest. The Torah records how these great men went wrong to demonstrate a woman's overpowering hold, and how sexual desire overwhelms even the greatest of men.[148]

A woman, though created differently, has many of the same inclinations as a man, only manifested differently. Today immorality has crawled its way into even the most protected homes. We think that we have guarded our homes against outside influences, but they still manage to get in. Let's not be naive by not talking to our children about things like this. Don't just assume that they know what is right and aren't exposed to the wrong side as well. Clarify matters for them; tell them how to deal with their sexual emotions. If you don't, you are more naive than they are! In a

---

142 Rabbi Nachman's Wisdom 115
143 Shevachay Haran 16
144 Ibid
145 Ibid.18
146 Sichos Rochel 1b
147 Imrei Pinchas HaSholem
148 Sefer Chassidim 225

society like ours, you cannot take chances. You must talk to your children and students. Tell them that the thoughts and temptations they might be having are normal, and only then tell them the words of *Chazal* on how to overcome the *Yetzer Hara*.

When you attain purity of the Covenant, you will have reached the highest holiness. When a person guards the Holy Covenant, it is as if he keeps the entire Torah.[149] The Holy Covenant makes a man's body radiant and lustrous, and one who guards it will never come to any harm.[150] For many years, *tzaddikim* searched for a *tikkun*, remedy, for sexual desire. It wasn't until about 200 years ago that it was found, but unfortunately, the remedy is not widely publicized. Rabbi Yehoshua ben Levi said: "Through ten expressions of praise, the book of Psalms was composed. They are: *Nitzuach, Nigun, Maskil, Mizmor, Shir, Ashrei, Tehilah, Tefilah, Hoda'ah* and *Hallel*."[151] These ten types of song also correspond to the ten *Sefiros* as alluded to in the Zohar. They, therefore, have the power to nullify the blemish caused by an impure experience. The ten Psalms a person should recite are 16, 32, 41, 42, 59, 77, 90, 105, 137 and 150, in the order shown. This is called the *Tikkun HaKlali*, the general remedy. "Every sin has its own remedy, but this is the general remedy".[152] Those struggling to overcome their sexual desires should say these Psalms. Those who seek a remedy for other problems should also say them, as they have the ability to rectify sins, even those we forgot about.

It says in the Talmud, "Sinful thoughts are worse than the sin itself."[153] Guard your thoughts very carefully, for thought can literally create life. The higher up a faculty is, the further its ability to reach. You can kick something with your foot, but you can throw it much higher with your hand. Your voice can reach still farther, calling to a person far away. Hearing reaches even farther. Father yet is the reach of sight, which can touch even the astronomical bodies. The higher a faculty, the farther it can reach. The highest of all is the mind, which can penetrate the loftiest heights. You must, therefore, safeguard your mind above all else.[154]

Our minds are constantly flowing with thoughts. Our minds jump from one thing to another as if having an internal conversation. The environment we are surrounded by very much affects these thoughts in one way or another. If you close your eyes you can see the mind at work; you will see images flashing before your eyes like a kaleidoscope. Controlling your thoughts can be difficult at first, but with practice and patience, it can

---

149 Zohar I, 66b
150 Zohar II, 3b
151 Pesachim 117a, Zohar III, 101a
152 Rebbe Nachman's Wisdom p.276
153 Yoma 29a
154 Sichos Haran 46

be done.

In the evening prayer service, we say that we will meditate on the Torah day and night. Extraneous thoughts are part of being human. I'm ashamed at my own thoughts sometimes, but I know that it's normal to have them. At the same time, I try to quickly change my thoughts, so I don't dwell on the negative thoughts. The second a negative thought enters one's mind he must immediately cast it aside with a good, upright thought. If this seems impossible at the time, one must cry out to *HaShem* from the depths of his heart.

The holy Seer of Lublin kept a strong practice from his youth: he would not think, speak, or do anything except what would give satisfaction or pleasure to *HaShem*.[155] When the *Rebbe* was young, he once traveled to be with his rabbi, Rebbe Elimelech of Lizensk. As he was traveling along, there was a very heavy rain, and it was dark and cold outside. He lost his way in the forest. Eventually, he saw a house with lit windows and entered it. It was warm and cozy inside and he felt relieved after having suffered so much in the cold and rain.

In one room he saw a beautiful young woman, and the *rebbe* didn't know what to do; it was forbidden to be alone with a woman. It also became clear that this woman was trying to talk the *rebbe* into sinning. She started telling him that she was unmarried and was ritually clean. The *rebbe* became very distressed by her enticements and her attempted seduction.

Though he was losing his composure, he at least remembered the fence he had made for himself and answered her saying, "I have accepted on myself not to do anything, not even something permitted, except what gives pleasure to my Creator. But what satisfaction will *HaShem* derive from this?" Just as he uttered these words, he realized that the whole scene before him was imaginary. There was no house, no forest, and no woman. He was standing by the road alone with not a person in sight.[156] It was all a test to see if he would be strong and control his thoughts.

Looking a sin in its face and running; that is how these *tzaddikim* became so pure. Rabbi Singer of Passaic said that it is specifically at these moments that we become great. Next time you face a sin, be strong and know that it's all a test. By passing this test, you will reach an all-new elevated level. Be strong! With the help of *HaShem*, you can overcome even the most difficult tests.

Iyov,[157] a very pious, humble man, was a clear target for *Satan*. Everything was going well for him, and *Satan* asked *HaShem* permission to test him. Iyov passed the tests and became even greater than he already was.

The Vilna Gaon says, "A person who is wise in his eyes will not

---

155 Seder Ha-Yom Ha-Katzar, P.12
156 Eser Orot, p. 89, #23
157 Job

make positive changes. Since he thinks he is correct, he is not aware of his negative behavior. But if a person knows what he's doing wrong, there is hope that he will correct himself".

One has to rise above his physical being and look at himself as with a mirror. One should learn *mussar* to help him do this. Through *hisbodedus*,[158] one can nullify his ego and thereby completely illuminate all his bad character traits.

Rav Levi bar Hama says, in the name of Rav Shimon bar Lakish, "A man should always incite his good impulse to fight against the evil impulse. For it is written, 'tremble and don't sin'. If he subdues it, it is well and good. If he has trouble, he should study the Torah. For it is written, 'Commune with your own heart'. If he still has more difficulties, he should recite the *Shema*. For it is also written, 'Upon your bed'. Should the negative impulse still affect him, let him remind himself of the day of death. As it says, 'And be still, *Selah*.'"[159] This advice from Rav Shimon bar Lakish should really be enough to help one overcome the *Yetzer Hara* but, since it is so tricky to defeat him, we need a little more advice.

If a person has erotic thoughts and cannot banish them from this mind, Rabbi Yehudah HaChassid has a few ideas to help this. "A person should try going for a walk until the thoughts go away, or he should talk to people about other things, or he should press his toes into the ground and place the full weight of his body on them."[160]

Another action a man can do to help fight his evil inclination is to purify himself in the *mikvah*. Rabbi Mordechai of Lechovitz said, "You should always seek to purify yourself in the *mikvah*, especially when necessary, for the *mikvah* purifies the mind.[161] The *mikvah* represents the womb. When an individual enters the *mikvah*, he is reentering the womb. Then when he emerges, he is as if born anew. From this, he attains a completely new status.[162]

It is said about the Baal Shem Tov, that he attained his enlightenment and great levels of holiness because he very frequently used the *mikvah*.[163] So here before you is clear evidence that immersion in the *mikvah* can help you fight your evil inclination; that is if you dunk in the *mikvah* with a yearning to attain levels of purity.

When a person gives of himself to others through charity and kind deeds, he will think less of himself and so is not as prone to sin. One's life should be devoted to helping others and he should not be centered only on

---

158 See chapter 6
159 Berakoth 5a
160 Sefer Chassidim P. 222
161 Zichron L'Rishonim, p.32
162 Rabbi Aryeh Kaplan, Waters of Eden, p.13
163 Keter Shem Tov, DhTvhY section on Taharah, p. 16b

himself. This will help balance his actions and thoughts. Charity protects against immoral fantasies.[164] It is also a remedy for immorality.[165]

The following advice can be found in Sefer HaMiddos in various places: Depression causes one to experience an emission. Eating garlic and eggs, engaging in idle talk or vulgar words brings on a wasteful emission of seed. A person who is afraid of immoral thoughts because of what he might see while walking through the marketplace should recite the verse, "Behold, the mighty ones will cry outside".[166] This will save him from the evil effects that come from his eyes having wandered. Gritting your teeth is a *segulah* against unholy thoughts. Gazing down at one's *tzitzis* has the ability to guard against sin. To chase away the evil inclination you should say, "*HaShem*, rebuke *Satan*". When a person studies Torah and performs acts of kindness he gains mastery over his inclination. Crying can also dispel immoral thoughts. A person should imagine his father's image. One remedy against evil thoughts is to become angry at something, as in Tehillim 4:5, "Become angry and do not sin." Ravi Nosan adds that the intent here is to become angry with oneself. This is hinted to in the teaching, "A person should always incite the anger of his good inclination against his evil inclination, because it is written, 'Become angry and do not sin.' This means to become angry with oneself but not to harbor real anger, which is a sin. A person can also leave the place where he is and go elsewhere. Just by changing the atmosphere, your thoughts can get a chance to regroup. Also, jumping up and down in one's place can help to get rid of wrong thoughts. Reciting the "seven voices" in Psalm 29 humbles the evil spirit. The light of a candle subdues the rule of the *kelipah*. All these things can help a person in times of panic to subdue his inclination." Please don't make these things a crutch for overcoming your desires; the true way is to work on yourself and nothing will protect you as well as the learning of Torah.

One's sexual desire is very much bound up with what he sees and hears around him. Try to stay away from situations that lead you to temptation and bad thoughts. Turning your face can be a simple remedy to avoid these problems, and also the thought that you are standing before *HaShem* always, "*Shivisi HaShem linegdi samid*"[167].

Sexual purity and mastery of the holy tongue are connected with each other. The more you speak with words of holiness, the more you will succeed in purifying yourself. In this way, you will also make amends for any immorality committed in the past. By the same token, the holier you become, the greater your mastery of the holy tongue. Each one feeds the other. You should understand that a similar relationship exists between

---

164 Likutey Etzos Tzeddakah 31
165 Ibid 32
166 Isaiah 32:7
167 See chapter 1

sexual immorality, *chas v'shalom*, and the abuse of language.[168] Reb Nachman says, "Be careful not to listen to the words of a person who is wicked and also intelligent. The mere words from his mouth to your ears can affect your soul. By actually speaking words of holiness on purpose, when attacked by improper thoughts, you can completely subdue them. The words one speaks are very powerful and can certainly influence him for good or for bad. The level of religious perception a person can attain depends completely on the degree of purity he achieves."[169]

A man once came to Rabbi Michel of Zlotchow, lamenting that he had inadvertently done something forbidden to do on *Shabbos*. He asked the rabbi what he must do for his *teshuvah* to be accepted. Rabbi Michel then explained to him the severe gravity of violating the *Shabbos* and that *Shabbos* is equivalent to all the other six hundred and twelve *mitzvos*. His sin was a very serious one, and he, therefore, prescribed for the man a stern remedy of fasting and self-mortification.

Later, this man came to the Baal Shem Tov, who told him that the fasting prescribed by Rabbi Michel was not necessary. Rather he should just provide the shul with candles. The man went out and bought candles made of tallow from animal fat, as that is what they were made of in those days. A dog then came and ate them, walking through an open door in the *shul*. The man then replaced the candles, but whenever they were lit they blew out. This he took as a divine signal that his *teshuvah* was rejected, and he told this to the Baal Shem Tov.

The holy Baal Shem Tov understood that the problem was due to Rabbi Michel's interference, as he believed that the stricter penance was necessary. The Baal Shem Tov then sent a message to Rabbi Michel, inviting him to come for *Shabbos*.

Accepting the invitation, the rabbi set out on the road Wednesday, to give himself time to arrive comfortably before *Shabbos*. The trip was constantly interrupted with one mishap after another. An axle of the wagon broke; a wheel fell off; the weather was stormy, and the driver got lost. Finally, Rabbi Michel arrived late Friday, right before *Shabbos*. When he walked into the Baal Shem Tov's home, he saw the *rebbe* in his garments, the table set, and immediately fainted. The Baal Shem Tov revived him and explained to this pious man that he had accepted upon himself the holy *Shabbos* a little earlier and that he had not violated *Shabbos*. He then said to Rabbi Michel, "When you thought for a moment that you had violated the *Shabbos*, how distressed were you? Don't you realize that, if the awareness that one has sinned causes a person to feel deeply distressed for having transgressed the word of *HaShem*, this is the true essence of *teshuvah*? There is no need for additional self-punitive behavior when regret has already

168 Likutey Etzos p.35
169 Ibid p.40

occurred. This man who came to you had already experienced pain from the awareness of having transgressed. Therefore, all that was necessary was a small action of penance because the true *teshuvah* had already taken place.

If a person has repented of a certain sin, and later reaches true perfection, he must still make amends for his earlier repentance. What he had achieved then was good only in proportion to the perception of G-dliness he had at that time. Now, after his repentance, his perception has undoubtedly increased. In comparison with his present perception, his earlier one turns out to have been very materialistic. He must, therefore, repent for the levels he achieved earlier because he had lessened the true exaltedness of *HaShem* to the level of materialism.[170]

One can see from this that *teshuvah* is something continuous. As we ascend the spiritual levels we realize how far from *HaShem* we truly were before. It says in *sefer* Hagilgulim that no two *neshamos* can be on the same level at the same time. As each person ascends a level, he can give the person above him a boost, which is why sometimes, even when we don't do anything extra, we suddenly feel uplifted, closer to *HaShem*. As we go up we can't completely forget the time we wasted below this level. We must ask *HaShem* from this new clarity of mind to forgive us as we realize more of the true hurt we have caused because of our sins.

There are many other characteristics the *Yetzer Hara* goes after in a person. We have centered on the main one; by defeating our evil inclinations with sexual purity, everything else will follow easily. When a person has one sickness, often the doctor treats the side effects and loses focus on the patient's main problem. Without a proper defense, one cannot defend himself in war. Whether you know it or not, you are at war with your *Yetzer Hara*. You must gather your plans of defense. To win you must understand your opponent's strategies. I hope I have helped you here to prepare your defense. Please don't forget that *Satan* is waiting for you to get depressed. When you do, this shuts down all your defense systems and lets him run all over you!

There is a reason why you personally, more than many of your friends, have such difficult tests to constantly face and overcome. You are not the normal run-of-the-mill person. *HaShem* has a lot of good things in store for you. The Zohar explains that, before salvation and good tidings, a person might experience hardship. It might seem impossible to handle what surrounds you on all sides, but you must always remember the powerful words the Baal Shem Tov said to his son: "My son, *HaShem* is always with you."

Abraham was a very important man with a bright future and therefore he faced tasks so difficult that few could pass them. Yitzchak,

---

170 Likutey Etzos 331,7

Yaakov, Moses, Dovid, Iyov and many other great people were stuck in situations where there was little light to illuminate their path, yet they held on. *HaShem* will always be in that light and so will complete salvation. What makes things more difficult is to see two lights instead of one. This second light sometimes glows from gold dust and only leads to nothing. This path is the easy way out, as it heads towards the gold color, but when you pick it up you realize the effort was all for nothing; the path was full of impurity, leading to sin and unhappiness.

Once we get used to running after gold dust it becomes very difficult to stop. Our Sages have said, one *mitzvah* leads to a second *mitzvah* and one sin leads to a second one. Once you fall into sin it becomes easier to fall into it again. Your mind becomes programmed to fall into the same trap over and over again. The only way out is to reprogram your mind. Next time, instead of reaching for the gold dust in the most trying, lowly, depressed situation, reach for the jewels! *HaShem* and the Torah are there for you. You must cling to them with whatever strength you have left. When *HaShem* starts lifting you up don't let go as you are so accustomed to doing. Reprogram yourself to hold on tight to your faith as you know you need to. Salvation is in *HaShem* and not in anything else. Know this in your heart and act upon it. Maybe you are feeling singled out by HaShem to go through such trying situations and the real truth is that you have been singled out. You have been chosen and I don't just mean to be a Jew with 613 *mitzvos*. There is something very unique about you personally. Inside you is a heart of gold and a longing to do good things for the world. Your soul has something extra holy and you have so much you feel you need to give. Therefore, you have been singled out more than others to be tested by *Satan*. If you want to win, search yourself for your good points. Make a list of these things in your mind or on paper. Don't give up and do not ever despair. When faced with the two lights next time, take the more practical one. Choose the light that will shine brightly for eternity and not just for a moment. It is there that you will find your deceased relatives and everything good. Go for the permanent fix rather than the imaginary, temporary one.

So, what do you do if you feel you are surrounded and you just don't have the strength? Then run! Escape in any way you know how in order to avoid the sin. The best place to run is to the Torah. If you can't get yourself to learn then leave the room and maybe take a walk outside. It was decreed that you face this situation at this exact moment, in this particular place, but if you leave it for a few minutes the urge to sin might completely pass. Do the best you can; you have a lot more strength still left inside you than you might think. Look at all the good things you do to serve *HaShem* and how you have helped others with your time and money.

Chas v'Shalom if you fail your test, you must know that *HaShem* is still there. No matter how far you may have fallen, He is there to sustain you. That is if you choose to let him. My friends, failure is common as we are only human beings made of flesh and blood. If you dwell on your sins they will only come to haunt you more. After making a mistake you must begin anew. This doesn't mean to forget about it completely, but for the time being, it might be best to put it aside in your moment of weakness. Pull yourself back up and then repent as soon as possible. Repentance should not wait, but it is not possible to truly repent while depressed. The fear of easily sinning again will only bring on a repeat occurrence. The Nikolsburg Rebbe once told a person who was scared of sinning again that he should just plain forget that it happened and not worry about it. He told this to him because the person was so wrapped up in worry that the worry itself was bringing on repeated sins ever stronger. Rebbe Nachman says if you believe that you can destroy, believe you can also fix. Sometimes the fix is to forget, while other times it is to remember.

The holy Baal Shem Tov was once taking a stroll through a deserted place. He had paid no attention to where he was walking since he was deep in his thoughts. He trusted *HaShem* that there must be some reason for being here, as everything in life serves a purpose. Suddenly he saw a huge frog. The holy Baal Shem Tov asked the frog who it was, and it answered his soul was a transmigration of a former scholar. His original soul had committed so many sins that it was forced to wander in this desert. The rabbi asked him how he sinned, so he could understand what had brought him to such a state. The frog said that, when he was in human form, he had once washed his hands carelessly. He didn't have the proper concentration and thought while washing and reciting the prayer. The deed rose up to the Heavenly Court. Of course, this isn't a terrible sin, but the negligence was bad enough that he had to do *teshuvah*[171].

Chazal teach us that one sin leads to another; the scholar didn't truly repent and was sent the *Satan* to test him in another situation. One incident after another, the scholar relaxed in his fear of *HaShem*. Soon became a great sinner. The Heavenly Court had now ruled that the scholar would not be forgiven unless he pleaded long and hard. The *Satan* once again came and induced him to drink so much that he could not possibly do any *teshuvah*, and the scholar continued sinning until he committed the worst of sins. When he passed on, it was decreed that his *neshama* transmigrate into the form of a frog. This was because his original sin had to do with water. He was sent to a deserted place so that no Jew would come along and recite a blessing, as that would elevate his soul and free him from this transmigration. After hearing his story, Rabbi Yisroel said the necessary blessings and praises to *HaShem* and enabled this soul to be saved, and the frog instantly died.[172]

---

171 Repentance
172 Sivchei Besht

Reb Nachman said that when you do *teshuvah* you must try and repent for the first time you sinned, and then all the repetitions of the same sin will be forgiven. No matter how deeply sunk in sin, this person could still have repented completely and never have been punished. *HaShem* was patient with him and gave him opportunities to repent. If only he had reflected and thought before washing his hands to concentrate better, he would never have sunk so deeply. We cannot ignore the trivial things we do wrong. We must confess and ask *HaShem* to forgive us, even for what we might think are minor sins: the failure to say a blessing over a cup of water, to skip the blessings upon rising from bed in the morning, and so on. As small as they might seem at first, each little thing can increase and thereby build a palace. As we taught above, a single *mitzvah* leads to another *mitzvah* and one sin leads to another.

Rabbi Meir of Premishlan lived at the foot of a very steep hill. Each day, even in the ice of winter, he would hike over the hill to immerse and purify his body in a stream on the other side. The people who knew of this considered it quite wondrous; they could only walk around the hill, afraid of falling on the ice. One day, a few young men decided to put an end to this superstition. Bravely, they followed the rabbi up the hill as he effortlessly ascended the once again. All the young men fell down and were badly hurt. What was Rabbi Meir's secret? "When you are connected above," he explained, "you do not fall down."[173]

If we want to fight the evil urge we must begin by connecting ourselves to *HaShem* throughout our day. Let us try to catch ourselves first before we fall. There are a few places of refuge: One is our faith in *HaShem*. Another is to surround ourselves with Torah thoughts. All this must be founded on a constant joy in appreciating all that we have from *HaShem*.

Rabbi Menachem Schneerson once said, "There is no such thing as defeat. There is always another chance. To believe in defeat is to believe that there is something at a certain point in time that doesn't come from above. Know that *HaShem* does not have failures. If things appear to get worse, it is only part of their getting better. We only fall down in order to bounce back higher."[174]

According to this thought process, there is no losing. Our failures, though not pleasurable, need not turn into depression and despair. In fact, a little reverse psychology wouldn't hurt now and then. Next time you fall *chas v'shalom*, bring yourself to elevated levels of joy! Be happy that *HaShem* has sustained you out of love for you. Let the joy radiate in your heart that you're going to come back even stronger in serving *HaShem*. There is no reason to despair; *HaShem* only wants to draw you close to Him and he hasn't let go of you. Now seek Him out and with joy make the necessary

---

173 Bringing Heaven down to Earth 129
174 Bringing Heaven down to Earth 139

changes in your life so this mistake doesn't happen again.

Our Sages said, "You have made man like the fish of the sea." Just as fish immediately die when removed from the water, so Torah scholars immediately perish when divorced from the Torah.[175] My friends, we have no strength without learning Torah. Our sages remind us, "I [*HaShem*] created the evil inclination and I created the Torah as its antidote."[176] I have heard these precious words for years, yet I still struggle to get myself to learn. With the help of *HaShem*, I learned another great approach from Reb Avraham ben Shlomo Zalman[177]! He writes that our rabbis said: "If this repulsive one engages you, draw him to the study hall. My brother, the *gaon*, explained, "If this repulsive one engages you" – this is the *Yetzer Hara*. When you are unable to withstand him because he overpowers you, then "draw him to the study hall." Tell him that in the study hall you will do his will by learning for selfish motives, in order to gain honor. This will put his mind at ease, and he will back down. Thus, "learning not for its own sake leads to learning for its own sake." In this manner, you shall free yourself from the *Yetzer Hara* completely. We understand the verse, "If your enemy is hungry" - and he desires to make you sin, "feed him the bread of Torah" - fulfill his will by learning for selfish motives, "for you will be heaping coals of fire upon his head" - when you subsequently reach the level of learning for its own sake.[178]

No matter what angle you take to help rid yourself of your *Yetzer Hara*, the final victory comes about through learning Torah. So instead of struggling day in and day out and wasting precious time over self-guilt, depression, anxiety and sickness, let us start curing ourselves! It's quite simple after all. Let us increase our learning of Torah!

As stated earlier, there are a few other major *taivos* but once the sexual inclination is under control these are easily solvable, as are many other negative traits. This chapter has mainly addressed just this issue. With *HaShem's* help, we will be able to purify our hearts and minds so as to be a vessel for the glory of *HaShem*. We all have the ability to reach the highest *madreigos* and they come about through *Tikkun Habris*[179]. Once purified, the holiness in our lives and hearts will shine so brightly that we will be on fire. We won't even think of anger or pride. Our hearts and minds will be at ease, yet we will fight to use every moment properly. The ego we once had will be nullified and forgotten. Our only concern will be for the portion of all the Jewish people and how we can help them draw close to *HaShem*. May it be *HaShem's* will that everyone discovers the strength we have inside us to

---

175 Maalos HaTorah p.54
176 Baba Basra 16a
177 The brother of the Vilna Goan
178 Maalos HaTorah
179 Purity of the covenant

serve *HaShem Yisborach.*

We are struggling because we are truly fish without water. Our souls are literally starving. Would we even think of doing such a thing to our bodies? How can we torture our souls like this? The *Yetzer Hara* is doing us a favor by pushing us around, because maybe then we'll wake up and see what is really going on. We are idle with our time and our thoughts. We are not putting Torah first in our lives; it comes last. Woe to us for not putting our foot down sooner and changing our ways! But it's not too late. *Boruch HaShem,* we are still alive and have time to save ourselves from *Gehinnom*[180]. Are we too lazy to become true servants of *HaShem?*

Here we have been spending hours a day in needless struggles, and we don't even know how much time we have left in this world. Maybe it's fifty years, ten years, one hour or even one-minute *chas v'shalom.* Do we want to end our lives, having wasted them with avoidable fights against our *Yetzer Hara?* If Torah comes first in our lives, then it's a whole other ball game. It is a completely different life, a life that tastes sweeter than the tastiest apple or orange. We walk around so bitter all the time, constantly searching for some sweetness to increase our happiness. What we fail to notice is what stands before us day in and day out: the Torah; and *HaShem* is watching our every move. Our father in heaven is wondering why his children don't take shelter in his wings. There is no comfort in the world other than in the Torah and *mitzvos* of *HaShem.*

In the mother's womb, a baby learns all of the Torah from an angel. Then, as the Midrash explains, the child forgets everything with a little bop the angel gives on the baby's mouth before birth. The child is supposed to forget the details in the Torah, so it should spend its time relearning in this world and fulfill all the *mitzvos* properly with effort. The baby is not supposed to forget that if its soul is hungry it should learn Torah. Of course, one's *Yetzer Hara* takes control when the Torah comes last. Making the Torah come first means that when you close your eyes at night you are thinking of a passage in the Torah and when waking up you yearn to begin your day, so you can do *mitzvos.* This level is not beyond us! It is just the beginning and is something we should not let slip away any longer. With *HaShem's* help, we will make a new beginning this very moment and start serving *HaShem* as we know we're supposed to.

Since the beginning of time, man has been trying to teach his fellow how to overcome his inclination. The advice I have given you will certainly assist in your battles, but will you overcome *Satan* and his tricks? I don't know. There is one piece of advice that I must leave with you, though. Much of your success in these matters depends on your willpower. If you want to be successful in life, you have to lay your cards out to

---

180 Hell

HaShem. With His help, there is no failure, but you must call on Him sincerely for assistance.

TEFILLAH FOR HATZLACHA

Master of the world, there is nothing in the world that can compare to You. You are far above all creatures, both on heaven and on Earth. To talk about You is to belittle all of the things you truly do and can do. You made man out of the simple dust from the earth. A woman you took from his ribs. From a drop of seed and an egg is created a wondrous embryo. Who is like unto You HaShem, Maker of heaven and earth?

I'm just a simple person, HaShem, yet I am tested as if I am a great man. What do I know of the Torah or of being a tzaddik? Yet every day my evil inclination works vibrantly to make me stumble in my ways. Well, I have to admit HaShem, I am striving, and I want to be a true servant, but these walls, how am I to climb them? Do I not hurt when I stumble? The only way to come close to You is to be tested. I am mere flesh and blood. I have flesh that bruises easily, and blood that runs hot inside of me. Do I mean to defile myself like those who have no covenant with You? I want to be true to myself and my Creator!

HaShem, I do not want to live a double life, one a life of Torah and the other a life of tumah. Our days here on earth are short. Before we know it, we will be standing before You giving an account of our every move in this world. What am I to say? Who will save me and explain that my intentions were good?

My evil inclination is smart. It knows how to push the right buttons and cause me to really mess up. The Torah is the antidote, but I haven't used it. I don't know why HaShem, I have no excuse, no reason to justify all that I have done since I was first created.

I have sinned by giving in to my inclination. Save me, help me escape my self-affliction. I don't want to end my days burning from the fire of Gehinnom. Instead, I would rather control myself in this world and not go after my physical desires.

Help me to falter no more, especially over impure desires. They are a striving after wind and give no true satisfaction. The only contentment is in Torah and good deeds. Everything else is fruitless.

Please help me to say the Tikkun HaKlali and may it purify every limb of my body. When I use the mikvah may it be with the true intentions of cleanliness in mind. Let my Torah learning be a true protection and antidote from all troubles. When I'm confused, help me run to you HaShem. Assist me in finding teachers I can confide in. One who will inspire me to repent - not only to tell me to repent but will also show me how.

HaShem, as You can see, I want only You. My heart might be confused but it is true to You. Take me back HaShem and rest Your Shechinah upon me. Forgive me, merciful HaShem. Thank You for all Your patience.

CHAPTER 4: TORAH STUDY

Whoever toils in Torah is considered to have offered all the sacrifices in the world. In addition to this, the Holy One forgives all of his sins." (Zohar 3:260)

Rabbi Eliezer ben Azaryah said, "If there is no Torah, there is no proper social conduct; if there is no proper social conduct, there is no Torah. If there is no fear [of *HaShem*], there is no wisdom. If there is no knowledge, there is no understanding; if there is no understanding, there is no knowledge. If there is no flour, there is no Torah; if there is no Torah, there is no flour[181]." If this chapter on Torah study were just to tell you how important it is to learn Torah, then it would serve little purpose - that is a given that has been taught to us by *Chazal*[182]. The true question is how to make the Torah part of ourselves, how to live and breathe the Torah and Judaism. To live a life of truth and fulfill our mission in this world: that is what our Torah study must bring us to.

I heard in a *shiur* given by Rav Mattisyahu Solomon: "If a person learns Torah and it does not become part of him, then he isn't learning Torah properly. A person has to internalize what he learns, and it must affect his will power. We have to want to make changes in our lives and in our middos. One can learn Torah all day long in *yeshiva* and get nothing out of it. We must repeat, pounding over and over again each <u>Torah</u> concept if that is what it takes to pierce our stiff hearts, full of *gashmius* and worldly ideas. One must learn something and then reflect upon it, letting his learning open up new doors of self-perfection and closeness to *HaShem*. Isn't this what Torah is all about?"

Rabbi Chaim Volozhin says, "This is the law of man. When a person busies himself with the Torah to observe all that he finds written

---

181 Pirkei Avos chapter 3.20
182 Our Sages

therein, he purifies his body from head to foot."[183]

It says in Sefer Yetzirah that the world was created with thirty-two mystical paths of wisdom. This is alluded to by the thirty-two times that *HaShem's* name, *Elokim*, appears in the account of creation in the first chapter of Genesis. The Torah is seen as the heart of creation. The Hebrew word *lev*, heart, is spelled out with a *lamed* and a *bais*. It so happens that the Torah begins with the word *Bereishis*, meaning 'in the beginning', which starts with *bais*, and ends with the word *Yisrael* (Israel), in which the last letter is *lamed*. This is to show that the thirty-two paths of wisdom are in the Torah and the numerical value of the word *lev*, heart is also equal to thirty-two. From this you can derive, if you do not let the Torah touch upon your heart, what have you accomplished?

There was once a couple in Russia who had trouble with their child, Mordechai. He never wanted to study Torah, only to play around outside. Mordechai also tended to get into trouble. This caused his parents a lot of anxiety. One day they heard that Rabbi Aharon of Karlin would be coming to their town. With a sigh of relief, they brought Mordechai to meet the *rebbe*. Rabbi Aharon listened to the parent's story and responded to them roughly. "I'll have a few words with your son and set him straight. Just leave him to me. I'll teach him how to behave." Mordechai's parents, taken aback by the rabbi's stern demeanor, yet assured by his confidence, let him take their precious son into his private room.

The *rebbe* leaned back on his couch and softly called Mordechai to come over; held out his arms and motioned for him to come nearer. Rabbi Aharon pulled the boy close and held him against his heart for quite a long time. Then they walked out of the room together. Not revealing the special method of persuasion that the *rebbe* used, he again spoke roughly to the parents. "I had a word with him. He'll shape up now!" The boy did indeed change his ways and became a well-known *tzaddik*, Rabbi Mordechai of Lecovitz, the father of the Slonim Chassidic dynasty. He always told his followers that he first learned Torah from R' Aharon of Karlin, who taught him Torah from the heart.

Torah is something very sweet. When it touches your palate, you must do as Rabbi Aharon of Karlin did when teaching it to others and yourself. The *rebbe* let it come from inside his heart. How did it get inside the deep chambers of his heart? He welcomed it through arduous work and through his great love and respect for the Torah.

Once your heart is touched, then what? If you do not put something into action and into real change, then it becomes stuck in your heart. Therefore, you must channel it into the right places, into the performance of *mitzvos* and a true change in your character. The Torah is

---

183 Nefesh Hachayim 21

not something just to think about. We must live it every moment and through every situation in our lives.

You might ask, where are the answers to all of my hardships? They are in the written and oral Torah. They are in the books and commentaries of our great sages, from how to wake up in the morning to how to fall asleep at night; it is all contained in the Torah. How does *HaShem* want us to live our lives? He wants us to arrange all our activities according to the Torah. The Torah is the blueprint of creation and our lives. It contains everything we need to know how to survive and fulfill our mission in life. Not only does it tell us stories of how our great ancestors lived their lives; it also tells us how to live ours today.

Some people think that the Torah's commandments were only required in the ancient days. They think this because they do not understand change and are missing the entire point of what Torah is. The Torah is a manual for life. It teaches us how to act and treat others. It explains to us how to find *HaShem* and how to find ourselves. Each commandment is a channel leading to truth in one's heart and for one's soul. As Rabbi Moshe Meir Weiss says, "The Torah is all good!"

"She is similar to a merchant's fleet, bringing her sustenance from afar."[184] Metaphorically, this verse alludes to the Torah, for *HaShem* provides for all the needs of those who study Torah day and night.[185] The comparison to a merchant's ships is very fitting because if *HaShem* wants a merchant to succeed, He guides him to a certain place, causes him to buy merchandise, and then induces buyers to come and buy his wares. In the same way, *HaShem* sends His angels from afar to give sustenance to those who devote themselves to full-time Torah study. That is why the Torah is called "bread" in Talmud Shabbos 120a.[186]

In the introduction to Me'am Lo'ez, Rabbi Yaakov Culi tells a parable: "Every person realizes that if a wealthy man or great scholar wrote him a letter that he should do something, he would certainly try hard to fulfill it as soon as possible. If the letter was written in a foreign language he would even be willing to pay for a translation, so he would know what to do. This should be all the more so in the case of the Torah, which is the letter from *HaShem* Himself!"

So how can we not devote our entire lives to understanding the Torah? Obviously, it is the will of *HaShem* that we do so. What could be better for one's soul and life than to learn Torah? Everything we do in life should be in order to study Torah, for is it not the air we breathe?

It is a *mitzvah* to teach Torah to our children, and it is also a mitzvah for us to personally learn it. If not now, when will we take to heart

---

184 Proverbs 31:14
185 Avodah Zarah 19a
186 Sefer Chasidim 208

our true purpose? When will we run our lives according to the Torah and reflect on it day and night as *HaShem* instructed in His letter to us? A home without words of Torah spoken in it is not a home. A synagogue in which people come only to socialize is not a synagogue. Rather, a gathering place for Torah learning is a true synagogue. The Talmud teaches us that when people learn Torah, especially in a group, the Divine Presence resides with them.

Reb Boruch of Mezhibuzh's young grandson, Yechiel, was playing hide and seek with one of his friends. Yechiel found a good hiding place and waited anxiously for his friend to find him. After a long while waiting, he looked around and realized that his friend had left. Indeed, his friend never even tried looking for him! Crying profusely, Yechiel ran and told his grandfather what happened. Reb Boruch also broke into tears. He said, "G-d says the same thing - 'I hide, but no one tries to find Me.'"

The life of a Jew is not supposed to be a complicated life. It is actually quite simple. A Jew is placed in a body in this material world for one specific purpose, to lift up the fallen sparks by doing various mitzvos. What mitzvah contains all others? The learning of Torah! How does one search for *HaShem*? To live a life of Torah and mitzvos is the only way one can find him. It says in the Zohar, "Whoever toils in Torah is considered to have offered all the sacrifices in the world. In addition to this, the Holy One forgives all of his sins."[187]

"Uncover my eyes that I may look upon the wonders of your Torah."[188]

Many people spend their lives searching in the wrong places. They do not realize that everything they need spiritually is in their own religion, Judaism. Rabbi Menachem Mendel of Kotzk taught, "There are many ways to approach *HaShem*, but most are dangerous. The only safe way is through the Torah."[189] Mysticism, mediation, music, and art are all part of the Torah. Science, astrology, and medicine can also be found in the Torah.

Rav Moshe Feinstein used to put his original Torah thoughts into writing. It is said that when a thought would come to mind and there was no paper around to use, he would record the *chiddush*[190] on any available substitute, even a stone. Rav Moshe learned Torah not only for the sake of the mitzvah but also with complete humility. In this way, he became the greatest posek of his generation. His sensitivity to others, guided by his love for Torah, gave him the understanding to make halachic rulings perfectly clear as Jewish society started to grow in modern times. Rav Moshe was very encouraging to his students. He felt that many times people did not

---

187 Zohar 3:260a
188 Tehillim119, 18
189 Emet VeEmunah p.12
190 Original Torah thought

reach their true potential, not so much by a lack of abilities as a lack of self-confidence.

In our day and age, many people lack confidence. We have little faith in ourselves and don't believe we can reach high levels of avodas *HaShem*. Our Rabbis constantly tell us the story of Rabbi Akiva and his wife, but we really don't take it to heart. Rabbi Akiva was a simple shepherd who barely knew a word of Torah, yet he turned himself around completely at forty years old. Not only did he acquire a life of Torah, but he also became one of the greatest rabbis who ever lived. How did he accomplish such heights? His wife believed in him, seeing that his heart was genuine. As he began learning Torah, he also began to believe in himself and devoted his entire life to learning and teaching Torah.

All my life I have tried to grow in Torah and Judaism. My father believed in me and because of that, I believed in myself. Let me be honest with you and admit I've had problems with self-confidence, but my father's belief is what helped me find it within myself. The support of my wife for writing this *sefer* also gives me the strength to finish this vast project. I tell you this so that you too should show all your friends and children that you believe in them. Of course, we should not need the encouragement of others; we should find strength on our own. We are just human, though, and today when self-confidence has fallen to an all-time low, we need those we love to show us support and respect. It is our job to encourage one another, especially those only beginning to grow in Judaism, but let us also not forget those who are already learning. They could use our appreciation to keep up their fine efforts.

It is written, "Water wears away stone."[191] What this means is that you should never give up on yourself and what you are doing. If you try very hard and struggle, eventually you will reach your goal. No matter how little Torah you know, the little you have is important. Can you imagine what you can accomplish in one year if you gave it all your strength? Rebbe Nachman says, "So many *tzaddikim* could have reached much higher levels if only they believed in themselves." Set goals for yourself in learning and serving *HaShem*; make things happen today. The Talmud in Sanhedrin says that with Torah study, you're even allowed to set deadlines for yourself and you will find it will help you succeed in completing many important works.

"Each day *HaShem* studies Torah for three hours."[192] If *HaShem* is the one who gave us the Torah, and He learns it three hours a day, how much more should we who received it from him. Many sages of the Talmud would not even walk four *amos* without reviewing a Torah concept they had learned. We should not be any different, especially those of us who devote countless hours in the *bais midrash*. If we spend so much time

---

191 Job 14:10
192 Talmud Avodah Zarah 3b

already learning in the *yeshiva*, we may as well continue thinking about it outside every moment we can. That is what gave these sages from the Talmud their energy and fire to understand and write some of the deepest *pasukim*[193] in *shas*[194]. They did not leave their learning in the study hall.

"The most important practice is that you think Torah thoughts not only when learning from a *sefer*, but also when the *sefer* is closed, to meditate on what you just learned. Doing this is not only to perform what is written, but also to purify and strengthen your mind. Is it not to your advantage in this world and the World to Come that, instead of allowing your thoughts to drift unrestrained, you ponder holy thoughts? And if it is too hard when you have some spare time to bend your intellect and think about complex matters like those in the Gemara, then why not think about pleasant matters from the *Aggadah* and books of *Chassidus* when you have a free hour or even fifteen minutes, and when you are walking on the road?

If in the beginning, this is difficult, then you should recognize that it is always easier to wallow in what you want than to hold yourself to some standard in the direction of integrity and piety. However, when you have accustomed yourself to this type of Torah meditation and have practiced it several times, you will not be able to walk around without holy thoughts.

After having kept up this practice, if it happens on occasion that you are walking on the street and stop meditating on Torah thoughts and holy matters as you go along, you might suspect that *chas v' shalom* you had actually committed a transgression of neglecting time put aside for Torah study."[195]

Have you ever noticed the fire in the eyes of a sage while he learns Torah? Do you know what that fire is? It is the glow of Torah. It comes to someone who learns Torah with much purity and love. One can work so hard on a *sugya* that he loses the simple enjoyment of the *mitzvah* to learn Torah. If it is not enjoyable to you, how will you remember what you learned? If you see a great sight and enjoy it, this affects your heart and you never forget it. The same is true with Torah learning. Therefore, let the joy of the *mitzvah* of learning become a strong part of you!

Have you ever realized that when your heart was filled with Torah, sadness could not find its way in? One's evil inclination puts all its strength into making a person think sad thoughts. Do you know why that is? It is because depression is the key *Satan* uses to unlock the door to get inside you. Do you know how to prevent this and fight back? Take him to the house of study, as our Sages of the Talmud advised.

I once noticed that every time I wanted to learn Torah, I would

---

193 Passages
194 The complete Talmud
195 Rabbi Kalonymus Kalmish Shapiro, the Rebbe of Peasetzna, Hachsharas ha-Abrechim, p.32

suddenly think of things I had forgotten to do. One time I sat down to learn and the next thing I knew I was at the sink brushing my teeth. Other times I would remember that I really should make some phone call so as not to forget. Sometimes I would sit down to learn and get a thought that I was hungry. I would close my *sefer*, eat and not return to my studies as planned. *Satan* has many tricks up his sleeve and, when you come to learn Torah, they all start manifesting themselves. If you watch out for yourself, you will see how obvious it is that *Satan* does not want you to learn Torah and perform *mitzvos*.

Once there was a rabbi who had a marvelous idea to protect himself from *bitul* Torah. Whenever he had a thought to go out and do something, he would first walk into the *bais midrash* and start learning a few minutes; then he would be able to think clearly. This way he was able to know if the thought was a trick from *Satan* to get him out of learning or if he should really perform this physical action.

Rebbe Nachman frequently stressed the importance of studying the Shulchan Aruch. He emphasized this more than any other study. It is best to study all four sections of the Shulchan Aruch in order, from beginning to end. If you can also study its major commentaries, it is much better. At the very least you should cover the basic work. This study is a tremendous spiritual remedy. When a person sins, good and evil are intermingled. A legal opinion is an obvious separation between the permitted and the forbidden, the clean and the unclean. When you learn religious law, good is once again separated from evil and the sin is rectified. The *rebbe* said that everyone must study the codes each day without fail.[196]

Do you know why our young scholars of today do not seem to retain Torah as those of previous generations? It is not that they lack enthusiasm; rather, they do not know how to channel their energies. Much of the answer to this lies in our present approach to study. The best way is to first learn all of Tanach; then Mishna, Gemara, and finally touch on Kabbalah. How do most of us study today? We put everything into Talmud or Kabbalah, and we wonder why we know nothing compared to the sages of the past. We have not learned sufficient Chumash and Mishna. All the Gemara stems from Tanach and Mishnayos, so doesn't it make sense to concentrate our efforts there first? Raish Lakish would review the Mishna forty times before he would discuss it with his teacher and comrade, Rabbi Yochanan.

I once asked Rabbi Shalom Friedman how Rabbi Chaim Vital was able to become a fitting vessel to learn Torah from the Arizal HaKodesh. He answered with a serious stare in his eyes, "Every day he immersed in the *mikvah* without fail. He began by learning Tanach; he followed this by

---

196 Rebbe Nachman's Wisdom, 29

learning Mishna. Afterward, he learned Talmud, and only then did he learn Kabbalah."

One problem people have is that, after their basic *yeshiva* education, they start learning less. As their lives get busy, they also lose their enthusiasm for learning. Since this happens so often, *yeshivos* see no choice but to push the learning of Talmud before *talmidim* are prepared. The philosophy is that the Talmud will at least sustain a person spiritually who most likely will be distracted by the vanities of this world and will only learn Torah a few minutes a day. There are many repercussions from this, one being that understanding true *pshat* is more difficult if not impossible. The learning of Talmud without all of Tanach and Mishnayos is not the way it was originally intended.

Today many have learned thousands of pages of *Gemara*, and they do not even know what happened in the book of Samuel. Others are scholarly in Shulchan Aruch with *smichah* but before having learned its source, the Gemara. Things are certainly twisted around a bit, but maybe that's the best we can do considering we have no desire to make time. Can you imagine, though, if we took the time to learn in the correct order? Maybe more of us would understand Torah as those of previous generations.

Our relatives up above are constantly looking down and praying for us. I wonder what they think when they see most of us wasting valuable time. They are probably thinking to themselves, "If only I could come down and tell them how much one *mitzvah* is worth in the next world. If only my great grandson knew what I know right now, he would stop chatting, do *teshuva*, and learn Torah properly!"

I am sure if our relatives could, they would tell us in our dreams that we have to be better Jews. It is for our nation that we must grow in Judaism. Think of our ancestors' struggles to keep Torah alive for all these generations. Sages have written thousands of *sefarim* in order to keep Torah alive. Some *rabbis* risked their lives to record their Torah knowledge and to publish their manuscripts. Today anyone can publish a book, but a hundred years ago? Many risked their lives to print words of Torah. We owe it to them to read these fine masterpieces they struggled and risked their lives over. After all, they did it just for us!

Some people limit the books of Torah they care to learn, but *HaShem* did not create *Chassidus* just for *Chassidim*. Nor did he bring the *Goan* of Vilna's Torah teachings into the world just for *Litvaks*. After all: He who is wise, learns from every man![197] Do you know how much you might be missing if you do not keep an open mind and learn Torah from many different pathways? A person should always choose one main *derech*, but if

---

197 Pirkey Avos chapter 4

he doesn't explore parallel teachings he is withholding much good from himself.

Many people who have never learned *Chassidus* in their *yeshivas* do not understand what it's all about. They think that *Chassidus* is basically Kabbala, extra knowledge not truly needed for serving *HaShem*, but *Chassidus* is something much different. It is something warm and sweet that brings a person to higher levels of love for *HaShem*, Torah and his fellow Jews. *Chassidus* is also spiritual concepts of Judaism, taught in a simple way that every man can understand.

What is the purpose of a teacher? His job is to take something above the student's knowledge and help him understand it in a straightforward way. This is what *Chassidic rebbes* have done. They have explained deep Torah concepts in a sweet and meaningful way. It would be an injustice to one's soul to not explore and appreciate these teachings.

Another way to view *Chassidus* is to understand that it is *mussar* from a unique angle all its own. It is not only for advanced students, as some have come to believe. The Baal Shem Tov *HaKodesh* is the sage who brought into the world the *Chassidic* movement. His intentions were that normal everyday people would be uplifted and serve *HaShem* more devoutly by it. The world needed more *deviekus*, fervor, and warmth, and the Baal Shem Tov knew exactly what was missing for the people. To know *Chassidus* is to love it! At the very least, one should respect and explore it somewhat. The Vilna Gaon, Rabbi Aharon Kotler, The Chofetz Chaim, Rabbi Yisrael Salanter, Rabbi Akiva Eiger, Rabbi Moshe Feinstein and many more have left us with their fine manuscripts on Torah. To not explore their works is also an injustice to oneself.

Rabbi Chaim of Volozhin once said, "Try to be as close to Torah scholars as possible, even if you do not understand what they are saying. This is analogous to a person who enters a store that has pleasant-smelling spices and perfumes. Solely by being in that atmosphere gives you a pleasant smell. So, also, you benefit by being in the presence of a Torah scholar, even if you do not grasp everything he says. Drink and thirst any words of Torah that you get the chance to hear."[198]

When the Rabbi of Lublin was a young man, he studied in the *yeshivah* of the holy *Gaon*, Rabbi Shmelke of Nikolsburg. Each time he was with him learning, he would smell the fragrance of the Garden of Eden. However, the *rebbe*, Reb Shmelke, would try to hide this and, whenever he studied with his *talmidim*, he had on the table various kinds of spices so that if one of them would detect something he would think it was just the spices.[199]

I would like to share how I got some extra help learning Mishnayos

---

198 Consulting the Wise, 4:18
199 Ohel Elimelech, p. 135, #343

from my father *zt"l.* To absorb the Torah, one has to toil and toil over it. Sometimes you get stuck in a place and cannot continue. As I was learning Mishnayos I became frustrated and did not know how I could finish the *seder.* I was ready to just quit and learn something else, but a sign was given to me. When I turned the next page, I saw a little strand of hair from my father's beard sitting in the crack of the book. I missed my father so much as he had passed away not long before but, through seeing a little strand of hair left there in my Mishnayos, I realized he too struggled over this exact *seder!* At that moment I cried and smiled. I was overcome by a new enthusiasm since I knew that the Torah I was learning was important. It was dear to my father's heart as it should be to mine. Wasting no time, I continued with this new vitality and thanked *HaShem* for showing me a miracle. As I moved from page to page over the next year, I always looked for another strand of hair, especially when the learning was extra difficult.

There is a special connection between a father and son, grandfather and grandson, especially when you walk in a place where your ancestors had been. Rabbi Shlomo Carlebach once said, "Only go to places where your ancestors have been before.

"Let me tell you: your relatives, maybe not one generation back but rather two or three, studied the Tanach, Rambam, Talmud and everything else they could find about Judaism. They were here before and they would love it if you visited the same places. My friends learn everything you can! Life is short and before we know it we will not be able to do any more *mitzvos.* Seize as many as you can and study very hard all of the Torah."

Once, Reb Shmelke (head of the religious court in Nikolsburg), was studying Torah with his holy brother Rabbi Pinchas. Both of them had remained awake together for a number of nights, studying while standing on their feet the entire time. Rabbi Pinchas could not find the strength to continue so he got himself a pillow to take a little nap. His elder brother Reb Shmelke reproached him, saying, "Brother! How can you stop learning the holy Torah, parting from something of everlasting worth for a transient pleasure?"

His brother Reb Pinchas responded, "Don't you see that I haven't the slightest bit of strength with which to continue?"

Reb Shmelke explained, "But I was speaking about just this moment that you used your energy to get a pillow for yourself. You could have applied that energy differently and remained standing and learning."[200]

As you can see, Reb Shmelke was so devoted to his learning and growth that he did not even waste one minute of his time that could have been spent learning. Not all of us will reach a level like that, but it's important to know that it's within our reach as well. The reason Reb

---

200 Mekor Chayim, p. 100, #333

Shmelke had such strength was not through the normal intake of food, drink and sleep. Rather, he was sustained completely by the Torah learning itself. This is the highest level of true learning and it is very powerful. Torah is so holy that the holiness it extends nourishes even the body like the purest of grains. To jump into learning at this level will only completely shatter one's body. A person must advance one step at a time. It is important to recognize the power of Torah. If only we comprehended it! Would we want to waste our days by oversleeping and talking idly?

Many of us struggle on a regular basis with our level of comprehension and memory. It can be frustrating to work hard at something, only to forget and not grasp it as you truly would like to. The great Gaon Rabbi Moshe Feinstein taught, "When you sit down to study Torah, clear your mind and experience a feeling of total newness towards what you are about to do. This will give you pleasure in the *mitzvah* of learning Torah. Just as a young child remembers well because his mind is fresh when he studies, so too you will remember what you study when you start studying Torah. This is especially important for people who are busy with daily activities. As you sit down to study Torah, clear your mind and you will then be able to concentrate with full attention."[201]

The technique of Rabbi Zusia's Torah learning was known to all. His pious way was to succeed at grasping all the difficult topics in the Torah just through tears and prayer. Once he was instructing a clever young man who asked profound questions the *rebbe* was not able to answer. The *rebbe* went into his room for a brief time; when he came out he gave an amazing answer, as if from one of the gaonim. During that time, he was not great compared to other *tzaddikim*. After this continued for some time, the astonished young man wondered how the rabbi came up with these incredible answers that so exceeded his level of Torah expertise; so he glanced through a crack in the door to see what Rabbi Zusya was doing in his room, and noticed that he was crying abundantly and hitting his head against the wall, and praying to the Holy One, blessed be He "Why don't You make known to me the wisdom of Your holy Torah?"[202]

If you do not understand a topic you learned, confess your sins, cry and give some *tzedakah*. This is a proven method and your eyes will be enlightened thereby.[203]

Many great rabbis have kept the practice of doing *teshuvah* before learning Torah. As it says in *Totzaos Chayim* pg.33, "Men of deeds make it an ordinary practice to come clean of their sins before they begin to learn. They do this is in order to eliminate the shells which darken the mind and inhibit them from understanding what they are learning." Some sages, when

---

201 Consulting the Wise, 8:2
202 Mazkeres Shem ha-Gedolim, p.68
203 Or Tzaddikim, p.16b, #17

getting stuck on a *halacha*, would remedy this by giving some *tzedakah* or performing some *mitzvah* and this would clear up their confusion.[204]

Rebbe Nachman says, "In the future *HaShem* will make everyone recall all he ever learned. This includes even things he forgot during his lifetime. It is true also of teachings heard from the mouth of a true *tzaddik* and not understood. In the future world, all will be comprehended. The Torah exists primarily for the soul. In the future life, all souls will recall and comprehend everything they listened to and studied in this world. Delighted is he who fills his days with much Torah and devotion."[205]

Rabbi Tzvi Elimelech of Dinov once said, "Prior to prayer and Torah study, after having done *teshuvah*, arouse your heart to fear *HaShem* based on your love for him. This is because, without such fear and love, the prayer or Torah you learn will not soar to heaven. You should arouse yourself by meditating on *HaShem's* greatness and exaltedness [to arouse fear and awe], and on all the abundant goodness he bestows on us [to arouse love]. During your study, continually pause just to meditate on this."[206]

The amount of learning one can accomplish when he has an ardent desire to come close to *HaShem Yisborach* is remarkable. Rabbi Gustman told his students, "The difference between us is that, when you have a difficulty, you just look around a little to see if the *Acharonim*[207] talk about a solution. If you can't find an answer quickly, you go off to eat, to sleep. When I have a difficulty, then there is no eating, there's no sleeping until I have found a clarification."[208] In Grudno, the town where Rabbi Gustman came from, it was not uncommon for a bachur to finish all of the Bavli and Yerushalmi Talmud by age sixteen, maybe even three times by the age of eighteen.

Every five months Rabbi Zelig Reuven Bengis, Rav in Yerushalayim, would make another *siyum* after completing *shas*. At the immature age of five, Rabbi Nochum Parzovitz knew the entire Chumash by heart. By eight he had mastered all of Tanach. The Machnovke Rebbe knew the entire Shulchan Aruch by heart but kept his talents to himself as much as he could. He would try to keep a precise schedule of learning each day; this included about eighteen hours of study a day. He also never missed an immersion in the *mikvah* for ten years while living in Siberia. When the Nazis, *yimach shemo*, were picking Jews off the streets, the Skolye Rebbe never missed going to the *mikvah* every morning. His gabbi would dress up in clothing similar to the Nazis' and pretend he was taking the Skolye Rebbe away. In this way, they were never caught and the *rebbe*

---

204 Zohar 1:185a Ibid p.32
205 Sichos Haran 26
206 Rabbi Tzvi Elimelech of Dinov, Hanhagos Adam #10
207 Post – 15th century commentaries
208 Torah Luminaries

continued his practice of attending the *mikvah* every day. How amazing it is when a person works on his nature so much that he becomes a breathing *sefer* Torah!

There is no one correct way for everyone to study. Many of our *rabbanim* have devised strategies to assist a person in his learning. For some a slower pace is best while for others a much quicker pace. One should never stop seeking the best methods for his study of Torah. The most important thing is to learn with all your heart and with proper intentions. This is within all of our capabilities. There is always more a person can learn; even after a lifetime of study one realizes he knows absolutely nothing. Coming to this realization might be the most crucial step in one's learning.

It is easy to get discouraged, seeing how vast the Torah is and how everyone around you seems like a master compared to you. These are normal feelings; we all have them. It is important to remember that the only opinion that truly matters is *HaShem's*. There is no race among students of Torah; there is no finish line or flag waving at the last lap. The scholar who wins is the one who practices and shares what he learns in a positive way. We are one nation and together we win. We learn this from the twenty-four thousand students of Rabbi Akiva who left this world early because they thought the Torah was 'about me'.

Many young scholars feel they are searching for truth in their learning by arguing about a concept as they would about points scored in a basketball game. When *Bais Shamai* and *Bais Hillel* argued about a *halacha*, it was not to increase their self worth. Having found the proper answer, they felt no pride. They felt no personal need to be correct. Rather, they were searching for truth and only the truth. Proper *machlokes*[209] is done *beshalom*, without hurting one's fellow Jew. Until the days of *Moshiach*, perfect truth is in exile but the person who finds it beforehand, by looking at the world with an eye of *shalom*, is praised.

In the old days, we used to be able to choose the *halachic* interpretation we wished to follow, *Bais Shamai* or *Bais Hillel*. The Gemarah suggests that a person should just pick one way or the other. That would mean holding by everything that rabbi taught, rather than pick and choose. In those days, one who retained the leniencies from both rabbis would be called wicked, while one who chose one rabbi and added the stringencies of the other was considered a fool. One day, a *Bas Kol*[210] came down and announced that we *pasken* according to *Bais Hillel*. Why? Because *Bais Hillel* was very humble. This Gemarah in Eruvin got me thinking how many of us pick and choose what we like in Judaism from different rabbis, and how doing this confuses us. Then again, we don't have rabbis the caliber of *Bais*

---

209 Disagreements
210 Divine message from Heaven

Shamai and Hillel. So, a *Bas Kol* came down to tell us to go with the humblest opinion until the times of the *Moshiach*. Maybe this is a hint to choose a *rabbi* who exemplifies this *mida.*[211]

Rabbi Elchonon Wasserman *hy"d* once said, "Torah means learning. Each word should contain a lesson; otherwise its place in the Torah is not justified." According to some opinions, one who is able to articulate the words when studying Torah but learns silently does not fulfill the *mitzvah* of Talmud Torah. Some *mitzvos* remain unfulfilled as long as we don't hear them in words.[212] Therefore, try to make sure your Torah study is articulated.

Most importantly, your Torah study should be purposeful. You should strive to study in order to perfect your character traits and draw closer to *HaShem*. The Torah was given to every Jew alike; everyone can study and benefit from this valuable gem! "The crown of priesthood Aaron merited taking. The crown of kingship David merited taking. The crown of Torah is still in its place. Whoever wants to take it, let him come and take"[213] I prefer the Torah of Your mouth over thousands in gold and silver.[214]

Every day for forty days, *HaShem* taught Moshe the Torah and he kept on forgetting it. Finally, on the 40th day on *Har* Sinai, because of his many merits, Moshe received it from *HaShem* as a gift. Therefore, keep doing the right thing; build up merits by performing *mitzvos*, study, delve into the Torah's beauty, and one day you too will receive a gift of Torah. The Torah was after all given to the Jewish people on the smallest of mountains.

The Midrash says that, when G-d was preparing to give the Torah, all the mountains stepped forward and declared why they thought the Torah should be given on them. "I am the highest mountain," said one. "No," said another, "I am the steepest mountain and therefore the Torah should be given on me."

One by one, they stated their claims. In the end, G-d chose Mount Sinai - not because it was the tallest or the grandest (it's not, as anyone who toured the Sinai Desert will attest), but because, says the Midrash, it was the humblest.

Great is Torah, for it gives life to its observers in this world, and in the World to Come. As is stated, "For they are life to he who finds them, and a healing to all his flesh."[215] And it says, "It shall be health to your navel, and marrow to your bones."[216] She is a tree of life for those who hold

---

211 Character Trait
212 Shulchan Aruch Harav, Talmud Torah 3:2
213 Yoma 72b
214 Psalms 119:72
215 Proverbs 4:22
216 Ibid. 3:8

fast to her, and happy are those who support her." [217] Woe to us for *bitul*[218] Torah, when our soul thirsts every moment for this comfort.

A *chatos*[219] is brought to *HaShem* on all holidays except *Shavuos* when there is no mention of sin with the offering. When a person accepts the Torah anew, deciding to dedicate his life to its study, the Torah itself brings atonement.[220]

HaShem wants to bring the Redemption... He is calling out to us, "Return to me and I will return to you.... I, only I am your beloved."[221] Ninety percent of people wouldn't sin if they had a true rabbi who they felt believed in them, someone available to them on a regular basis whenever needed, with whom they could make a personal connection.

Do you believe in your spiritual potential? If you get rid of the physical distractions and exterior evils that have attached to you, you are left with a 100% pure soul. That pure soul is connected to *HaShem* and is capable of understanding all of the Torah. It is able to grow into a *tzaddik*. The only thing holding it back is your belief in your true potential, thereby rising above negativity.

In the days of Yermiyahu people were complaining they didn't have time to study Torah since they were too busy earning a livelihood. To answer their complaints, the prophet instructed someone to go into the Aron[222] and view the manna that Aharon *Hakohein* had been told to hide there. Then he held it up and said, "See this manna; it should remind you that *parnasa*[223] only comes from *HaShem*."

Once I was borrowing a friend's Talmud because I couldn't afford my own. When the day came that I acquired my own set of *Shas*, I opened up the new book to the exact *daf*. I was on. The volume I was studying had hundreds of pages. What were the chances I would open to the exact page? So, I wonder: can we even ask if there is One *HaShem* in the heavens and the Earth; One *HaShem* Who looked into the Torah and created the world? Do we really expect *HaShem* to make His Presence even clearer to us, when it is obvious every second that He sustains us?

---

217 Ibid 3:18
218 Wasted time
219 Sin offering
220 Talmud RH Yerushalmi 20b
221 Jeremiah 4:1
222 Ark of the Torah
223 Sustenance

PRAYER FOR TORAH STUDY

Thank You, HaShem for giving me the strength and time to learn. I am grateful that You created me as a Jew and have given me one mitzvah equivalent to all 613 commandments. A mitzvah is so precious to me that I am pleading with You, HaShem, to allow me to fulfill it in all of its particulars, learning Torah for its own sake and without ulterior motives, to study with joy and serenity. Please give me shalom with those around me so I can concentrate and not be distracted. Please HaShem, take away the worries of parnasa and give my family sufficient income so I can devote myself to Torah study.

Ribbono Shel Olam, help me please to teach and practice the Torah I learn so it won't be lost. Help me understand and remember everything I learn so as to fulfill it in all its aspects.

The Yetzer Hara is constantly on the chase to prevent me from learning. Instead of me failing to strengthen myself as I should, let Satan fall from his attempts at preventing me from study. HaShem, I truly want to study Your Torah and I do not want to waste away my days in pointless, frivolous things. I know that I can do better HaShem but not without Your constant assistance. HaShem, I am calling for help from the deepest depths of my heart. Honestly HaShem, it's not that I don't know how to serve You and overcome my evil inclination. I do know! I'm being realistic by asking for Your assistance, as I am sick of failing You HaShem, my forefathers, parents and myself. I can try fooling myself all I want, but when it really comes down to it most of my problems stem from bitul Torah. Master of the world; help me to use my time properly from now on, not wasting one minute on unimportant things. Torah is first, Torah is last, and it is true happiness!

I appreciate Your patience with me HaShem. You have watched over me even when I was undeserving, and You have saved me countless times. No one in the world could ever care for me as much as You do. When I stumble, You are there to lift me up. When I rise up, You are there to grasp me in your light. Without You HaShem, I am nothing.

CHAPTER 5: HUMILITY AND SIMPLICITY

Shlomo HaMelech says, "The goal of knowledge is to realize one's own ignorance." (Chovos HaLevavos 1:10)

Rebbe Nachman once said, "My achievements came mainly through simplicity. I spent much time simply conversing with G-d and reciting the Psalms." Through these basic actions, which can be performed by everyone, he accomplished a great deal. The *rebbe* yearned to serve G-d like the unlearned, common people. He would often say, "Oh! Oh! Simplicity!" The *rebbe* spoke with many *tzaddikim* who all attributed reaching their high *madregas* (spiritual levels) through absolute simplicity. They would do the simplest things, secluding themselves and conversing with *HaShem*. This is how they attained what they did. "Happy are they."[224]

Rebbe Nachman explains that one should follow the Code of Jewish Law with simplicity. "One does not have to be a genius to serve G-d. All that he requires is simplicity and sincerity."[225] Every good and holy thing can be done with absolute simplicity. "One can study much Torah, do much good, and spend much time in prayer, all without sophistication at all."[226]

When Reb Dovid of Zelin saw his friend, the great Rabbi Dovid of Lelov, he called out excitedly to his wife, "We must prepare a special meal for an honored guest." Her cupboard bare, she was disappointed that she would have only bread to serve. She kneaded the dough and made simple biscuits. After eating, the distinguished guest complimented the hostess heartily, "These cakes are exceptional." Upon his return home, the rabbi commented to his wife about the wonderful biscuits he ate while visiting his

---

224 Sichos Haran 154
225 Shevachay Haran 13
226 Rebbe Nachman's Wisdom 19

friend. "They truly had the flavor of *Gan Eden!*" Surprised at this comment, the *rebbetzin* went to the wife of the Rabbi of Zelin to get her secret recipe. Approaching the marvelous cook, the *rebbetzin* said, "I never heard my husband get excited about food before. The biscuits must have been extraordinary. Please give me the recipe." Her friend, a little embarrassed, began to explain, "When my husband told me that your husband was coming, I was very happy. I wanted to prepare something special for him, as it is not often we have a *tzaddik* visit our humble home. Besides, he is my husband's good friend, but all I had in the house was a little flour."

"So, what did you do?" asked the *rebbetzin*. "I *davened* to *HaShem* and said, '*HaShem*, You know if I could, I would joyously prepare the most delicious and elaborate meal for such a *tzaddik*, with no expense spared, but since all I have is a little flour, *HaShem*, would You please put some of the taste of *Gan Eden* into my baking in honor of our guest?'" Delighted, the *rebbetzin* responded, "That is exactly how my husband described it! He said it had the flavor of *Gan Eden!*"[227]

Who binds Heaven and Earth together? The *tzaddik!*[228] He is above the physical world, yet he is not; nor can he ever be as spiritual as G-d. Through the *tzaddik*, we have a bridge we can use to get close to *HaShem*, but we must be close to the *tzaddik* to draw from his spirituality and advice. By being close to a *tzaddik* one can learn true humility. Simplicity and humility go hand in hand. Moshe, the greatest leader of men, said of himself that he was a humble man[229]. His love and devotion for *HaShem* were based on complete simplicity.

When the Gerer Rebbe Rabbi Aryeh Leib first took leadership, some *Chassidim* wanted to see what the new *rebbe* was all about. When they came the *Rebbe* said, "So you've come to spy out the land? You will recall that, when they finally met Joseph, his brothers did not recognize him, thinking he was an Egyptian. Now is it not strange that the righteous Joseph could be mistaken for an Egyptian? The answer is simple: a real *tzaddik* like Joseph is able to conceal himself to the point that he can be mistaken for a gentile..." From that moment on, the *Chassidim* all became followers of the Gerer Rebbe.[230]

There are many stories of sages who kept their devotions secret, so people would not realize their high *madrega*. Some separated themselves from society as much as possible to serve *HaShem* privately. Some took on a position as *melamed* of small children, a job lowly as a water carrier or *shul* custodian. Why did they need this secrecy and what did it accomplish for them? The way to come close to *HaShem* is through *bitul* (self-nullification).

227 Why the Baal Shem Tov Laughed 31
228 Zohar III, 257a
229 Bamidbar 12:1,3
230 *Rebbes* of Ger, Artscroll Books

When a person thinks of himself as being *bitul*, he is joined with *HaShem*. We are his creation; compared to him we are absolutely nothing. Shlomo HaMelech says, "The goal of knowledge is to realize one's own ignorance."[231]

The *rabbis* teach that with one *mitzvah* it is possible for a person to reach the highest levels. Without humility and the realization of lowliness in comparison to *HaShem*, we can't possibly come close to him. Becoming like nothing means knowing that everything comes from *HaShem*.

Although humility brings a person to the World to Come, humility itself does not exist there. In the World to Come, no person will be able to honor his fellow by saying, "Sit beside me." Each person to repose in his place and each one comes in peace to the place that has been prepared especially for him. If a person humbles himself in this world, though he has the opportunity to progress and attain dominance, he will occupy first place in the World-to-Come.[232] An example of this is the *B'nei Beteira*, who resigned their leadership in favor of Hillel.[233]

The pious sage Reb Elimelech once said that he was assured of a place in the World-to-Come. When his time would come to go up to the world above and he would be asked if he had studied Torah to the best of his ability, he would answer "No"; if he had served *HaShem* fully through worship, he would say "No"; if he had completed his quota of *mitzvos* and good deeds, he would say "No". Then they would say, "If so, then you are telling us the truth, and in that case, you deserve reward in the World-to-Come."

Once I was telling a friend about the troubles I experienced and all the things I felt lacking in my life. He gave me a deep look and said, "Who are you to think you deserve anything more than what you already have?" His voice was so strong that it penetrated my heart. I told him that his remark was true, and I thanked him, even though it was difficult to accept at the time. This person was *samayach bechelko* after losing one wife and soon after another. I learned how to appreciate what I have by seeing him live so simply and humbly. He lives with the thought that he already has been blessed with more than he deserves.

Tzaddikim who keep their pious actions secret are called hidden *tzaddikim*. This is one of the highest levels among those who serve G-d. The aspect of secrecy promotes the *middah* of humility in them. The great *rebbes* of former times understood that their holy devotions did not need to be public knowledge. Maybe the world was not ready for their light to be revealed. Eventually, though, many *tzaddikim* were found out or had to come into the open to help the world. There are many wonderful stories

---

231 Chovos HaLevavos 1:10, Lekutey Maharan 24:8, Paparos LeChochmah on gittin 47a, Shevachay Moharan 8a, Sichos HaRan 3a
232 Bava Metzia 85b
233 Sefer Chassidim

about *tzaddikim* that show us how we should act.

Rebbe Nachman says that stories of *tzaddikim* have the ability to wake a person up, even if he is stuck in the deepest pit of depression or idol worship. The holy Baal Shem Tov said that stories of *tzaddikim* are equivalent to *Miesa Merkava*, one of the deepest kabalistic concepts. We do not tell enough stories, considering their ability to wake us all up.

I don't know about you, but I feel especially enriched when I hear stories about the greatest sages who practice humility. It is one thing to be humble when many people are smarter than you but take a *tzaddik* among the elite of the generation. How is it possible they can be so humble about themselves?

Rabbi Yochanan ben Zakkai received [the oral tradition] from Hillel and Shammai. He used to say: If you have studied much Torah, do not claim special credit for yourself; for this very purpose you were created.[234] This is not such an easy achievement but our *rabbanim* have lived up to this expectation many times.

Rav Yisrael Abuchatzeirah, known as Baba Sali, was famous for his humility. He would often say, "Woe to those who believe in someone who is nothing." He would express vexation after everyone left and ask, "Why do they come here? What do they see...?"

Rabbi Shmelke of Nikolsburg arrived in a town where he was soon to be greeted by a multitude of his followers. Before meeting the crowd, he asked for a room where he could take some moments of solitude. One of the *Chassidim* was curious as to what the master was doing in seclusion. Putting his ear to the door, he overheard his *rebbe* say, "Welcome to our city, honorable *rabbi*. It is our privilege to have you here. Thank you, holy *tzaddik* for coming for a visit." The Chassid later asked Rabbi Shmelke to explain this strange practice. "It is simple," the *rabbi* said. "I anticipated what my followers would exclaim to me. I, therefore, said it to myself first, and it sounded so foolish that when they said it to me later, it appeared equally ridiculous."[235]

Rabbi Chaim Shmulevitz would open up a Gemara, turn the pages and read during a *shiur*. Those standing behind him sometimes noticed that the *sefer* was not even turned to the correct page. Reb Chaim knew the text completely by heart but, in his humility, he made it look as if he were reading.[236]

An upstairs neighbor of the Gerer Rebbe, Rabbi Simcha Bunim Alter, came home to find a note on his door stating that his daughter could be found with the family Alter. He quickly rushed downstairs to find out if his little girl was okay. When he came into the Alter house he saw the *rebbe*

---

234 Pirkei Avos 2.9
235 Not Just Stories p.300
236 Rabbi Chaim's Discourses

sitting in the kitchen, offering the little girl sweets to comfort her, after finding her crying in the hallway![237] From this, we see that a *tzaddik* would even make time from his busy schedule to care for a little girl who was crying. He did not find the feelings of others, even a child, beneath him; in fact, quite the contrary. One can never be too holy to do kindness after all that is what holiness and Torah are all about!

When the mighty mountains heard that *HaShem* planned to give the Torah from a mountaintop, they began arguing amongst themselves. Each of the mountains felt it was best suited for this event. Mount Tavor, Mount Carmel, and others claimed that the Torah should be given upon it.

"You are all mountains but none of you is fit," said *HaShem* to them. You are so lofty that you are filled with pride." Mount Sinai, lowest of the mountains, stood by silently during all this debating. Seeing this, *HaShem* declared, "That is the mountain on which I shall give the Torah, for only it is fitting." It is humble and also the place where Yitzchak was bound as a sacrifice to *HaShem* when it was part of Mount Moriah. Therefore, it deserves the honor more than all the rest and that is where we received the Torah![238]

We learn Torah from our sages for the same reason. The sages are humble; therefore, people listen and respect their teachings. We must emulate their ways; the only correct paths! One cannot come close to *HaShem* when his heart is full of pride. The mountain was chosen only for its humility; we too will be chosen to enter the highest levels only for our humility.

There is one thing that our holy *rabbanim* have always had in common, the willingness to do anything for *HaShem Yisborach*. Some of our holy masters mortified themselves through fasting, while others took axes, broke the ice in a pond and immersed[239]. If they did this once in a while maybe we could comprehend it, but friends these acts were done constantly. Others took upon themselves to remain silent for forty days. There were even some who locked themselves up in a room for months. It's funny; we have all of these stories that tell of these Rabbis' devotions, but let me ask you: do we really know? Can we even begin to comprehend the holiness, love of *HaShem* and self-control these *tzaddikim* had?

Some people think that holiness is a gift you are born with. Those people are sadly mistaken. *Tzaddikim* earn every ounce of holiness they attain. The question is: how do they attain self-mastery and how can we reach the same plane in our lives? If your desire is strong enough, you are willing to do anything for it. The same has to be true of Torah. If you ask

---

237 Torah Luminaries, Artscroll
238 Shabbos 89
239 Immersing in a stream, lake or mikvah can purify a person from damage done through sins and can help a person reach very high levels of holiness.

any scholar, he will tell you that you have to be willing to go through the wall, so to speak. That is what these *tzaddikim* are all about. They want to come close to *HaShem,* and not only that; they are persistent in making it happen.

Self-control is everything. Do you think that when the Baal Shem Tov stood at the lake ready to immerse, he did not have a second thought telling himself that the water was too cold? Having self-control though, he overcame these thoughts and completed the action for *HaShem.* We have to do the same in our lives. Let us not move over and let our bodies do the driving. They will only steer us off the road and into a ditch. How will we get out then? Our *rebbes*[240] will have to pull us up! Better we should let our *neshamos* do the driving. Our *neshamos* are experienced and familiar with the roads ahead that we need to follow. What is this road? It is self-mastery, doing the will of *HaShem* and thereby fixing our *midos*[241]. That is what these *tzaddikim* were all about, putting the *neshama* in the driver's seat, following the Torah straight ahead!

Your *rebbe* in *yeshiva* can give you the Torah, yes, but only you can turn yourself into a *tzaddik.* You have to ditch the way of the world, even the way, unfortunately, of many of your Jewish friends, and you have to follow the Torah. The Torah will not come after you, nor will self-mastery. If you want it you have to go after it, making Torah first and foremost in your life.

Do not let your eyes, ears, and mouth control you. Take back control over yourself. Protect what you have. Do not let your ears hear what is bad for you. You cannot let your eyes run freely either. Let's not have our palates touch food that is wrong for them. Most importantly, let us take back our minds.

We are told that, in our day and age, mortifying oneself is not the best way to come close to *HaShem.* Various practices of self-mortification did help *tzaddikim* of the past to reach their levels, but our bodies are not as strong as theirs were to handle such practices. In our day and age, there is so much impurity to get into. Just to stay away from an improper movie, too much television (or any for that matter), literature not based on Torah, the internet, a pool hall, sports games and who knows what else. I could go on, but I probably have already touched a nerve in you and myself. *Chazal* say, "Whatever character traits and things are most difficult for you to overcome, this is your true test in life."

It is said that the generation of today can reach the level of the great Rabbi Akiva. To do so though, you must believe in yourself and take control over your life. People cannot perfect themselves without being in control of their time. Stay above your body and yourself; give to *HaShem*

---

240 Another term for *rabbi,* teacher and guide
241 Character traits

and to others. Also know that, when you say a *beracha*, it truly makes a difference and shakes the heavens. Do everything with love and with all your heart. Rabbi Shlomo Carlebach said, "If you don't do something with all of your heart, you're not really doing it." That is what made these *tzaddikim* who they are. All of their devotions: the ice, fasting, Torah study, and prayer were done with all their hearts. To help a fellow Jew out, enjoy it and give it your all; that is true life. The harder the test, the greater is the reward.

HaShem wants us to strive to come close to him, yet the vanities of this world hold us back. Why do we let them? How can we allow the impurities of the world into our homes and our lives? What is worse, we neglect taking steps for our children's protection. By the time we realize we let down the gate that protected them, they are already lost. We have to make sure that we are not pushing our children away, instead of pulling our children closer. This is a common mistake. The best approach is to teach love of *HaShem* and his *mitzvos*. This is done by example. There is always hope, as no prayer goes unanswered and no effort goes unnoticed.

Our physical bodies constantly desire the pleasures of this world. This is because *HaShem* created us with free will, so he could see if we are true to his commandments. If a person sees things that are holy, the holiness rubs off on him. Spending time with *tzaddikim* is of tremendous benefit to the soul. A person is strongly affected by his surroundings. For this reason, a man wears *tzitzis*, to remind him of the *mitzvos*. It is written: "You will see it and remember all the commandments of G-d and do them."[242] This world is a tricky place, *tzitzis* are the only reminder that a man sees on himself at all time to remind him to turn away from evil and do good.

The holy Baal Shem Tov said, "Attach your thoughts to above. Do not eat or drink excessively, but only to maintain your health. Never look intently at mundane matters, nor pay attention to them, so you may separate from the physical. Intent viewing of the mundane brings coarseness on oneself."

Just like surrounding oneself with a holy atmosphere helps a person perform more *mitzvos*, surrounding oneself with unholy things can lead a person to sin. Rashi says, "The eyes see, and the heart wants, and the body commits the sin."[243] Gazing at physical and mundane desires will arouse a person to sin. Our sages of blessed memory thus said: "Sight leads to remembering and to desire." It is written of the Tree of Knowledge that it is "desirable to the sight and good for eating..."[244] The sight of it made it desirable.[245]

---

242 Numbers 15:39
243 Ibid. 15:39
244 Genesis 2:9

The Baal Shem Tov comments on the saying: "Turn aside from evil and make good."[246] This means that you should make the evil into good.[247] In everything you do, *HaShem* can be found. Everything physical in the world around us contains sparks from above. It is our job to elevate these sparks by thinking about who created them and using them to perform *mitzvos*. Even the worst sinner has a spark of good in him. All this can and should be turned around to good. Generally, the higher a person's *madrega* the more he is able to lift up these sparks. Those who are farthest from *HaShem* and return are his dearest's as it says, "In the place where those who repent stand, even the perfectly righteous cannot stand."[248]

Man's main task in this world is to transform darkness into light[249]. The truth is, though, that even bad is actually good; how could *HaShem* really create something bad? It has been taught that these sparks fell from the time of the world's creation. To bring the Final Redemption, all the sparks must be elevated back to their source. May it be soon in our generation that together we complete these final elevations!

To do so, we have to not only perform the commandments but also do them out of love. Serving *HaShem* through fear is the level of a servant and serving him from love is the level of a son.[250] *HaShem* wanted servants, so he created the *malachim*. He wanted children, so he created *B'nei Yisrael*.

One final thought on simplicity and our role as students and teachers:

Rabbi Yisrael of Ruzhin was traveling through all the places where the Baal Shem Tov had been during his youth. The rabbi came to a village that stood between Kitov and Kossov and asked the Jews who lived there if they remembered anything about the holy Rabbi and how he conducted his *avodas HaShem*. They referred him to an old man, a gentile who had been the mayor of the village. Rabbi Yisrael found him lying in bed, infirm in his old age. He asked what he knew of the holy Rabbi Yisrael Baal Shem Tov. The man began to share what he remembered: "Regardless of the weather, the Baal Shem Tov would immerse himself in the nearby stream. Once when I saw him, I noticed that his feet were stuck to the ice; as he tried to remove them blood flowed from his feet. From that day onwards, when he would go to immerse and was under the water, I would go and pile straw on the place where he emerged. I kept doing this for him for a long time until one day the *rabbi* thanked me and asked me with what I wished to be

---

245 Tzava'as Harivash 5-6
246 Psalms 34:15
247 Keter Shem Tov 69
248 Berakoth 34b
249 Zohar 1:4a
250 Kedushas Levi, Yisro. p. 36

blessed with. The *rabbi* offered me long life, wealth or honor. I did not want to give up any of these blessings, so he blessed me with all three.

"It later became known among our town that the waters of the stream had miraculous healing powers and people flocked to bathe in them. I became rich from the use of the stream and was honored by the people by appointing me their mayor.

"I had asked the Baal Shem Tov one last thing: 'How long will I live?' The Baal Shem Tov kindly responded, 'You will live until a sage comes to you bearing the same name as I, having a similar appearance, and you will tell him about me.'"

Rabbi Yisrael of Ruzhin bid him farewell and thanked him for his story. Before leaving the village, he was informed that the old man had passed on.

A storyteller is called a *maggid*. Many of the old Jewish towns had *maggidim* known for their stories. One contemporary *maggid*, Rabbi Pesach Krohn, has published books and tapes. The greatest *maggid* of this generation was Rabbi Shlomo Carlebach, who used to travel around with his guitar and tell stories in his finely-tuned singing voice. People from all over the world would gather to hear him tell stories and sing. He woke many religious and non-religious Jews from their sleep. People far from the traditions of Torah would turn over a new leaf, all because of his stories. Reb Shlomo would tell of simple folk who served G-d with all their heart, sometimes inspiring an audience of thousands.

Rebbe Nachman said Stories have the power to wake a person up spiritually. When it comes to learning how to be a simple and humble person, the best thing to do is to read about others who followed these traits. Then you too can follow their example and become a remarkable human being.

Every one of us can be a *maggid*. To our children, friends, and spouses we must tell stories. One book called Rebbe Nachman's Stories contains deep, purifying stories written by divine inspiration. The *rebbe* said that even a barren woman might finally conceive by hearing these stories. To mention all of them here would be too vast a project, but I do recommend reading them and other exceptional stories of the sages.

TEFILAH FOR SIMPLICITY

HaShem, You appreciate even the simplest acts of man and thereby return a reward to him. Your mercy is unending. How can I thank You for the good You bestow on me?

We are taught it is not the complicated acts that You seek but those performed with a realness of heart. There is nothing like a simple Jew who completes a mitzvah with love. I want to love you with a simple love. Please show me the way to reach true devotion. Guide me on the path to simple, wholesome love.

Help me to see myself as in a mirror, to know how to correct my deeds. Draw me close to You, HaShem. All I want is to come close to You. "Bless me with love, grace, loving-kindness, and mercy in Your eyes and the eyes of all who see me."[251]

HaShem, what a pleasure it is to be a drop in the ocean, part of the people You call Klal Yisrael. Thank You for giving me the mitzvos and the privilege of being Your servant. Please send me mitzvos I can perform with love, so I can give back to You whatever is in my ability.

---

251 Prayers From the Heart p. 422

CHAPTER 6: HISBODEDUS, MEDITATION

"Each night I meditate in my bed." (Psalms 6:7)

Hisbodidus is the practice of spiritual meditation performed individually for the purpose of drawing close to *HaShem*. Almost from the beginning of time, people reached an elevated level of *avodas HaShem* – service to G-d - through *hisbodidus*. Without this private, personal communication with one's Creator, it is unknowable how even the greatest sage could come close to *HaShem* and grow spiritually. This practice is the root and foundation of holiness and repentance, above all else. Therefore, *hisbodidus* should become a standard practice for all.

When first learning about *hisbodidus*, many people realize they have been using it either consciously or subconsciously for years. Whether walking or sitting in rush hour traffic, one might naturally start talking in his own words to *HaShem*, expressing his personal troubles. Sitting alone at night affords the best opportunity to start conversing with *HaShem*. Rebbe Nachman teaches that *hisbodidus* is the highest path of all, and he encourages everyone to reserve an hour or more each day for this purpose. Considering our over-scheduled lives, it may seem hard at first to set aside this time. However, the benefits that come as a result far outweigh the time spent.

Rebbe Nachman suggests, if possible, that one meditates alone in a room reserved for Torah study, prayer, and meditation with *HaShem*.[252] If you do not have a special room available, you can still meditate and converse with *HaShem*. A man can create his own special room under his *tallis* by draping it over his eyes, thus secluding himself from his surroundings. One can also sit with an open *sefer*[253] and, instead of studying, speak to *HaShem*.

---

252 Sichos Haran 274
253 Book

Dovid HaMelech used to practice *hisbodidus:* "Each night I meditate in my bed."[254]It was a comfortable and private place where he could reflect and pour out his heart to *HaShem.* Moshe Rabbeinu went out at midnight and spread his hands to *HaShem.*[255] He went into a private place and meditated in prayer. Some people prefer to meditate in a quiet field, alone with nature. The Baal Shem Tov used to practice much of his *hisbodidus* in the forest where it was quiet and secluded. The atmosphere itself is beneficial to this process. It is taught that every blade of grass has a *malach*[256] above, watching it grow.[257] When talking to *HaShem* in such a place, surrounded by the grasses and the *malachim,*[258] a person's *hisbodidus* reaches an elevated state. The *malachim* take on the role of messengers; they help elevate one's words and, in a sense, join in one's prayer.

Hisbodidus is the key to *mussar*[259] and coming close to *HaShem.* Every moment of *hisbodidus* is precious to *HaShem*; this simple devotion can lead a person to the greatest levels of spiritual purity.[260] Although our greatest *tzaddikim*[261] have utilized *Hisbodidus* to reach their elevated *madregos*[262], every person regardless of age or degree of observance can employ it. Ironically, people completely removed from Torah who do not routinely pray will often practice *hisbodidus* to get close to *HaShem* in their own personal way.

Unlike formal prayer, *hisbodidus* is an individual's personal communication and should be spoken using one's own vernacular. There is, however, a basic formula to *hisbodidus* that empowers a person's prayers to draw *HaShem* close. It is best to do it at the same time each day, preferably at night, after *chatzos.*[263] At this time, the world is asleep, but the gates of heaven are wide for our prayers to enter. As it is written, "By day *HaShem* will command His mercy, and at night His song is with me."[264] The truly righteous are awake when the rest of the world is fast asleep. Our minds are also clearer spiritually, so we can think about our lives with the utmost clarity.

One of the goals of *hisbodidus* is to nullify one's ego and selfishness. At first, a person should talk about every little thing important to him, trying to focus primarily on his *avodas HaShem.* He should tell *HaShem* about

---

254 Psalms 6:7
255 Brachos 3b
256 Angel
257 Likutey Maharan 2:11, Rebbe Nachman's Wisdom#163
258 Angels
259 Character correction
260 Hishtap'kus Hanefesh, Outpouring of the soul #2
261 Righteous people
262 Spiritual level
263 Midnight
264 Psalms 42.9

each character trait that needs improvement. It takes practice, introspection and many sessions of *hisbodidus* to present oneself before *HaShem* with complete humility. *Baruch HaShem*, practiced the right way, *hisbodidus* will lead a person to the level of *bitul*. When that occurs, one's heart will burn with love and fear of Heaven to such an extent that nothing comes between him and *HaShem*. A person's mind will be focused with clarity that he never experienced before, and performance of *mitzvos* will take on a new meaning and passion untouchable by the *Yetzer Hara*.[265] Every day will be one of spiritual growth and purification. No *sefer* or *drasha*[266] will do anything for a person unless he applies this learning in a practical and productive way. One hour a day of reflection, thinking and speaking to *HaShem* about one's life and the world around him is all that is needed.

One of Rebbe Nachman's main tasks in this world was to remind us the importance of this overlooked devotion. He said, "One who does not meditate cannot have wisdom. He may occasionally be able to concentrate, but not for any significant length of time. His power of concentration will remain weak and cannot be maintained. A person who does not meditate won't realize the foolishness of this world. But one who has a relaxed and penetrating mind can see that all around him is vanity."[267]

For some of us talking to *HaShem* in our own words is easy, while for others it can be a struggle. Even throughout our lives, at certain times it will come naturally while at other times we find it difficult. At times we might sit in our special place and draw a blank, unable to think of anything to say. We might find that the spot where we did *hisbodidus* previously only brings us to a lack of concentration. Move to another place when this happens, but do not give up. Sit in a new place and repeat the words, '*Ribbono Shel Olam*' (L-rd of the Universe) and 'it is still very good'.[268] Even concentrating on one word will allow a person to remain mentally strong. Repeat that word over and over; meditating on that single word is itself very good. *HaShem* will show his mercy and open one's mind and mouth so he will be able to express his thoughts.

My friends, I know from the bottom of my heart that *hisbodidus* has helped me in ways I cannot even express. It does wonders for my soul and increases my *emunah* and *bitachon*[269]. There was a time in my life when even the simplest things I tried to accomplish were insurmountable. I gave in to laziness, sleep and became too impatient to do *hisbodidus*. I had to fight my way back to practice it regularly and, when I did, I no longer complained over the hardships of my life. I could unburden myself of the difficulties

---

265 Evil inclination
266 Sermon
267 Rebbe Nachman's Wisdom #47
268 Tzaddik 440
269 Trust and faith in *HaShem*

and struggles I was experiencing; I became content with my family, friends and myself and they found me easier to be with as well. If I committed a sin, I removed the pain of having done so by confessing to *HaShem* during my *hisbodidus*. My health and emotional stability improved. I felt nullified before *HaShem* and this helped me realize that my life should be devoted to *HaShem* alone. Rav Noson said, "You can be sure that if you had hisbodidus for 40 days straight you would see a change for the better."[270]

Chazal teach us that *HaShem* helps a person to follow the path he wants to follow[271]. If the path in your heart is Torah, *HaShem* will help you follow it and nothing will stand in your way. If you push yourself to do *hisbodidus* for an hour a couple of times, it will be easier to incorporate into your daily routine and you will succeed. You might attain such a degree of happiness and contentment that an hour of *hisbodidus* each day will not be enough; on your own accord, you will want to add more time. As with anything one finds good in his life, you will want to teach this wonderful practice to others and, *im yirtza HaShem*, you will. When Rav Noson zt"l first heard this teaching from Rebbe Nachman he said, "I'm going to go out and scream this in the streets and tell the world that I know the secret how to come close to *HaShem*." The *rebbe* responded, "They won't listen to you; you have to teach it carefully."

The Jewish people knew that the Torah and commandments were true and said, "We will do as we have heard."[272] I'm not asking you to take my word for it; see for yourself how *hisbodidus* will give meaning to your *avodas HaShem*.

When formulating our prayers, the Great Assembly tried to begin each section with praise to *HaShem*, and only then to beseech him for our needs. We begin *Mincha* (the afternoon service) with the prayer of *Ashrei*, which is full of praise to *HaShem*. We end *Mincha* with the prayer of *Aleinu lishabeach*, which discusses our obligation to praise. Our *hisbodidus* utilizes the same format, starting with praise, then our personal topics of introspection, repentance, fulfillment of physical, material and spiritual needs then, finally, more praise.

A person must pray for everything. If for example, a person's garment is torn, and he has no money to replace it, he should pray for a new one. One should pray for all his needs, large and small. *HaShem* gives us food, clothing and everything else we need, even if we don't ask for them. We are similar to the animals in that: "*HaShem* gives food to every living creature" [273], but a human being must receive all of life's necessities only through prayer. Rabbi Nathan once mentioned to Rebbe Nachman

---

270 Aveneha Barzel p. 66 #43
271 Yoma 38b
272 Exodus 19:8
273 Psalms 147:9

that he needed something small. Rebbe Nachman instructed him, "Pray to *HaShem* for it."[274] It is important to ask *HaShem* for all of one's needs. Do you need a new car? Is your dining room table broken? Are you struggling financially? It doesn't mean that, when you ask *HaShem*, the requested items will magically appear on your doorstep. He might help you get an increase in salary or a better paying job. You may find that an item you've needed is on sale at a price you can afford, and to make it easier, you might get a check in the mail you were not expecting. Some people would attribute this sequence of events to "coincidence", but we know in our hearts that it all came together because *HaShem* orchestrated it for our benefit.

There is an old joke about a man who had complete faith in *HaShem*. It started raining heavily and the river overflowed, flooding the streets. The man's neighbors came banging on his door and shouting for him to evacuate his house, but he refused, saying, "I'm waiting for *HaShem* to save me." The water rose above the first floor, so he went to the second floor and sat by the window, waiting. Rescue workers came by in a boat, urging the man to join them in the boat, but he refused; he was going to wait for *HaShem* to save him. The water continued to rise, and the man had to climb out the window onto the roof of his house. A helicopter came by with a ladder thrown down to the man. The pilot shouted for him to grab the ladder, so he would be saved, but the man stubbornly refused. With no place left where he could wait for *HaShem*, he drowned. His day of judgment came and *HaShem* asked why he drowned. The man said, "I had complete faith that You were going to come and save me, so I refused help from all the people." *HaShem* replied, "Who do you think sent your neighbors, the rescue workers in the boat and the helicopter pilot?"

Although we must have faith that *HaShem* will send what we need, we have to be aware when it arrives and accept it. The things we need don't have to come wrapped in a miracle to show that *HaShem* sent them. Sometimes it can be difficult to see the hand of *HaShem* in what we receive, but it's always there.

Are we supposed to think that *HaShem* has no idea what we need unless we ask him for it? Of course, he knows! The purpose of asking for the things we need and want isn't, so we can get them fulfilled. Rather, we have to ask *HaShem*, so we can recognize that everything comes from him. When do most people resort to prayer? Given the nature of human beings, when everything is going well when we have everything we need and want and are healthy, we forget to acknowledge *HaShem's* hand in keeping order in our lives. He sends us troubles and difficulties specifically, so we will pray. If you do not plead to *HaShem* about all your problems and needs, you might miss the point of the difficulties you're experiencing. Turn to *HaShem*

---

274 Outpouring of the Soul #36

for everything. We must pray for His assistance, put our faith in Him and be patient. Only *HaShem* knows what is best for us. We might pray for something that we think we need, but we don't get it. The natural reaction is to think *HaShem* didn't answer our pleas. He always answers us, but sometimes the answer is no or something else that is better for us. Maybe you asked for a new car because the car you're driving now is old and lacks the newest comforts and technology. Nothing occurs to allow you to get the new car, so you assume that *HaShem* ignored your request. In fact, in his infinite wisdom, *HaShem* sees that if you get that car you will drive to a certain place at a certain time and he knows that at that time and place there will be a fatal car crash. By saying 'no' to your request for the car at this time, *HaShem* is saving your life.

Something occurred quite a few years ago that sends a chill up the spine of anyone who hears the story: A couple rented a house not far from the husband's job, where he was a mid-level executive. They were expecting their first baby and wanted to buy the house. They worked out terms of the purchase and signed a contract. One day, the wife called the landlord/owner in tears: Without warning or reason, her husband lost his job. The couple didn't know how they would buy the house, let alone manage with a baby on the way. The owner told her not to worry about the house; they could suspend the contract if necessary. More importantly, the owner told the wife to realize that although she couldn't see the reason at this time, her husband did lose his job for a reason and something good would come of it. Approximately two weeks later, a local restaurant burned down; there were no survivors. It was reported on the news that the people who died in the fire were all managers of the company from which the husband had been terminated. Had he not lost the job, he would have lost his life. The owner called the couple to see how they were faring. The wife was again in tears, but this time tears of relief that her husband was spared, and she would not have to raise their child alone. He found a new job at a higher salary in a new location and they moved.

Frequently we don't get what we pray for but should still pray for things we feel are important to *avodas HaShem*. Whatever it is, no matter how unimportant it may seem, pray to *HaShem* for it. Take all your health, money and family problems, offensive neighbors, whatever is causing you hardship, and lay it all out to *HaShem*. Pray for help in your devotion, to be worthy of drawing close to him.

People often think that *hisbodidus* is done mentally, without speaking. This is not correct. Some people have the mistaken impression that they are supposed to shout to *HaShem*. It is important to talk quietly to *HaShem* and listen to what you are saying. Thinking positive thoughts is always beneficial. *Hisbodidus* should be practiced in a modest way. The entire purpose of this practice is to become completely *bitul* - nullified.[275]

Therefore, it is best done privately, and few people should know the exact time your devotion is performed.

When a person does *hisbodidus*, he should choose his words carefully and think before uttering each word. At the same time, speaking to *HaShem* should be as comfortable as speaking to a close friend. Rebbe Nachman teaches, "When a person speaks to *HaShem* and uses every kind of argument and appeal to 'conquer' *HaShem*, then *HaShem* himself has immense joy and pleasure from this. He will send words to this person's mouth, so he will be able to 'conquer' *HaShem*. How else could flesh and blood win a victory against *HaShem*? It is only because *HaShem* himself helps us."[276]

Hisbodidus follows the format of our conventional *tefillos:*[277] Starting with praise, followed by requests. One should express his thoughts and troubles to *HaShem* like a child complaining to his father.[278] "You are children to *HaShem*."[279]

Praise *HaShem*. You might wish to say, "*HaShem*, thank You for creating me as a Jew and giving me the opportunity to serve You. You do so much for me that I often overlook it and take it for granted. Even when I sin, You sustain me and allow me to repent. There are no words sufficient to praise You. If all the seas were ink and all the land paper, I could not possibly write down all the praises I owe You." Your personal *hisbodidus* should be your own words brought out from the recesses of your heart.

The body of *hisbodidus* will differ with each person. It should cover introspection, repentance, and prayer for one's physical and spiritual needs.

Speak about your day, narrating what you did and how you handled situations that you faced. By going through the events of your day and how you dealt with them, you will be able to improve your *midos*.[280] Discuss with *HaShem* the difficulties you face and how you might improve in the future. After reflecting on your day, you might wish to occasionally reflect on past days.

Ask *HaShem* to forgive your sins and mistakes, recounting them individually. You should even discuss a simple thing like having omitted *modeh ani*[281] in the morning or having said it without the proper intention and ask *HaShem* for help.

Review your whole life with *HaShem* on occasion; try to recall events for which you might not have repented completely. This way, you

---

275 Likutey Etzos, Hisbodedus 6
276 Likutey Etzos, Hisbodedus
277 Prayers
278 Rabbi Nachman's Wisdom #7
279 Deuteronomy 14:1
280 Character traits
281 Modeh ani is a prayer said as soon as one awakens in the morning

will remove all Divine Judgments against yourself. Your fear of *HaShem* will be pure, not clothed in phobias. You will not be drawn down by self-recrimination because you know that you have placed your sins before *HaShem*, as Dovid HaMelech taught, "My sin I make known to you."[282]

Go through your attributes such as anger, pride, depression, lust, jealousy, hatred, laziness, etc. This part of *hisbodidus* should be done with the intention of nullifying one's ego and surrendering oneself to *HaShem*. Begin with one-character trait such as anger and stay there as long as possible to cover all its aspects. This way you can truly reflect on your errors and make the necessary changes.

You might wish to say, "*HaShem*, anger is a character trait that leads a person to sin. When people lose control over themselves by getting angry, they hurt themselves and the people close to them. Anger causes a person to be sick from constant anger in his heart. *HaShem*, I have such a problem and I'm not sure how to rid myself of it. I get angry quickly and barely have time to think of a way to save myself from this anger. I'm always upset with my wife and friends and this takes me far away from You. So many people are being hurt by my anger; this pains me. *HaShem*, I need Your help to stay calm and think first. Help me emulate Your ways; You are slow to anger even though we challenge You on a regular basis. I'm asking for Your assistance, so I can do better and deal with situations in a more appropriate manner. Someone once tested Hillel to see if his being asked ridiculous questions over and over would anger him. Hillel did not lose his temper. I want to follow in the ways of Hillel, our sages, and You, *HaShem*."

When you have completed talking about one topic, go on to the next. After thoroughly exploring each character trait, you will find yourself completely refreshed with new confidence in your ability to make necessary character changes. Soon you will feel yourself become *bitul* before *HaShem*. Self-reflection in the form of *hisbodidus* is valuable for our *midos*.

Now that the basics are covered, you are free to talk about your spiritual and physical needs. Spiritual needs are most important and should take precedence, but a person's physical needs must not be neglected. When talking about spiritual needs, set your heart on fire and beg *HaShem* to draw you near to Him. Tell Him your struggles in trying to serve Him and how you want to be infused with his holiness. Appeal to *HaShem* and tell Him how you want to learn Torah for its own sake. Make your way through the *mitzvos* you want help to fulfill. Tell *HaShem* all that you want to accomplish and how much you want to come close to him. Pleading with *HaShem* to attain spiritual heights is holy and purifying. Yearning and praying are not enough; after *hisbodidus*, we have to work hard to attain what we want.

---

282 Psalms 32:5

Don't forget to pray for the spiritual and physical wellbeing of the entire Jewish nation. This thought should come naturally if one has properly nullified his ego through some of the above practices. The Talmud teaches us that if you pray for another person who is lacking what you are lacking, you will be answered first.[283] How much more so should you pray for the needs of all Israel in which you too are included. When you want to pray to *HaShem* for something, meditate on your soul as part of the *Shechinah*, Divine Presence.[284]

Having addressed one's spiritual needs, it would be an appropriate time to go through all of one's physical needs. Your physical needs could include your health, job, home, car, clothing and any other item you're lacking. Rebbe Nachman once saw his student Rav Noson wearing an old pair of shoes. He told him, even for such a small item, you should pray.

We end *hisbodidus* in the same manner as we started, with praise. For example, "*HaShem*, thank You for giving me the opportunity to speak to You about my needs. I can't thank You enough for being there for me through all my ups and downs. Without You, I would be lost. You care so much about every one of Your creations. I know I have not begun to open up my heart properly to You, so I hope You will help me to do *hisbodidus* again soon. Thank you, *HaShem*, for drawing me close to You and hearing my prayer. There is no one else besides You, that can help me. 'You open your hand and satisfy the desire of every living thing.'[285] *HaShem*, I love You and Your Torah. Thank you for giving your nation a way to draw close to you and the Torah."

The importance of practicing *hisbodidus* daily should be obvious now. It would be unfortunate to not take advantage of this gift from *HaShem*. There are many vital messages you should have received from this chapter: The first is to pray for everything. Reb Nachman Chazan was once hammering a nail; the hammer slipped and hurt his hand. Reb Noson said to him, "Why didn't you practice *hisbodidus* before swinging the hammer? You should have prayed to hit the nail and not your hand."[286]

The second message is that *HaShem* is with us at all times, waiting for us to ask for help. Third, *hisbodidus* is the vehicle with which many *tzaddikim* reached their high *madregos;* it can help you do the same. I hope you understand the importance of making *hisbodidus* at a set time daily, not rushing through it in five minutes but taking at least one hour to really examine, reflect, think, and meditate. You will develop peace of mind, knowing that the Creator of the universe wants to hear from you and help

---

283 See chapter on Speech and Prayer
284 See chapter on Speech and Prayer
285 Psalms 145:16
286 Siach Sarfei Kodesh I-687

you. Most important is that you pass this teaching to everyone who might benefit from it.

TEFILAH FOR HISBODEDUS

The Torah You have given us is so precious and dear. When it's cold outside I still feel your Warmth. As much as darkness manifests itself in the night, there is so much light from shining Your mercy.

Every day when I wake up I'm created anew. Unfortunately, I don't feel very new. This is not Your fault, HaShem, as I am the one who takes little time to reflect on the things that I should. This is why I need to start a regimen of hisbodidus into my schedule.

HaShem, I try to do hisbodidus, but it seems like the channels to Heaven are blocked for me. This is only a mirage – a false vision from my imagination - but being mere dust and ashes, I lose hope and lose patience with my prayers. I am begging You for help. I know the gates are open for me, though I choose to ignore them. Help me set aside a proper time for hisbodidus and during those times please hold open the gates of Heaven and help me pour out my heart to You.

Assist me, HaShem, to say the right things once I start speaking, to pray for all my spiritual and physical needs without confusion as to what my real needs are. Help me to confess all my sins of today and mistakes of the past. Let my ego be nullified as I stand before You, pleading to be forgiven while drawing closer to You. Let me not forget the needs of others during my prayers. HaShem. You give me so much hope and joy and I feel so loved. Aid me please in expressing my true love and feelings for Your commandments. Don't allow days and weeks to pass with my plate remaining empty. Thank you, HaShem, for teaching me about hisbodidus. For this alone I'm indebted to You.

CHAPTER 7: ARISE

"Arise, call out at night, at the beginning of the watches." (Eichah 2:19)

For more than two thousand years the Jewish people have been exiled from their home. The holy city that once flourished is surrounded by controversy, strife, and bloodshed. Our Holy Temple stands no longer, and we are left with one beautiful wall to remember her by. The *Kohanim* and *Levi'im* are unable to perform their service in the Temple. The Jewish people have fallen from the loftiest heights, no longer basking in the warmth of the *Shechinah*.

We are so worried about our own lives and troubles that we forget the pain of others and the pain of *HaShem*. The Holy One, blessed be He, created the Torah and *mitzvos* and gave them to us as a gift. He gave us a way to come close, yet we continuously forsake Him and add to His pain. Just imagine the sweetest person giving you a precious gift, worth millions, and from your anger, you throw it back at him. Why are we so angry with *HaShem*? Why do we hurt the One who truly loves us the most?

It is within our power to bring an end to this exile from the real Jerusalem. Our nation has been exiled for so long that we don't even know what we're missing. The land as we see it today is not as *HaShem* promised it would be. Our return to Jerusalem will only come through our return to *Yiddishkeit*, Torah, and *mitzvos*. At that time, the righteous *Moshiach* will come and our return will soon follow. The land will no longer be desolate and bare but will flourish like it did over two thousand years ago. Our Holy Temple will be restored, and evil will dissipate from the world. The dead will arise; everyone will be at peace.

The first exile was caused by the sins of idol worship, illicit relations, and murder, and was redeemed in the merit of Avraham, Yitzchak, and Yaakov. Our present exile was caused by the sin of *loshon hara* and baseless hatred, the antitheses of Torah[287]. This exile will end through the merit of Moshe and the Torah that was given through him.[288]

There are many teachings on what we must do to bring the final *geula*. Some important aspects of redemption are that Jews from all over the world will return to their Jewish roots and follow the *halacha*. Rav Yochanan said in the name of Rabbi Shimon bar Yochai, "If the Jewish nation keeps two *Shabbosos* in a row, *Moshiach* will come instantly."[289] Another aspect is to rid ourselves of baseless hatred among different groups within the Jewish people, as well as our neighbors. Rabbi Menachem Mendel Schneerson taught that learning about *Moshiach* and the laws of the Temple hasten *Moshiach's* arrival. All these aspects are important in hastening the final redemption.

There is a special devotion that has the ability to hasten our *geula* that is unknown to many. It is a devotion that is so holy that many people who practice it keep it to themselves. To some, it was the most important religious devotion they performed. The simplest Jew to the greatest *kabbalist* would in the middle of the night break the slumber of their eyes and awaken to say the holy prayer of *Tikkun Chatzos*.

Tikkun Chatzos is a prayer that speaks of the yearning for redemption from this long and bitter exile, the pains of *HaShem* and the Jewish nation over the loss of the Holy Temple. When saying this prayer, one is prone to tears over the hardship of our nation and the loss of the Temple. Each of these tears from reciting *Tikkun Chatzos* rises heavenward and is very dear to *HaShem*. *Chazal* teaches us, "In the merit of those who mourn over the Temple, the Temple will be rebuilt." By reciting this special prayer, one is not only taking responsibility for his sins and those of the generation, but also the sins of past generations. Could there be a greater show of love and yearning for spirituality than the recital of this prayer? The Zohar says, "All our suffering in this bitter exile is caused by not getting up to study Torah and sing songs of praise after *chatzos*."[290]

You may think, "Who am I to pray over the exile and Jerusalem? Will the in-gathering of the exiles and the final salvation come about because of my prayers?" The answer to this is the same as we have learned.[291] "The reason why each individual is created uniquely is so that each one will say, 'The world was created for me.'" It gives *HaShem* great delight when his children pray and entreat him about this, even if their request can't be granted because the time has not arrived or for some other reason. Even so, they have done their part and *HaShem* rejoices over this.[292]

---

287 Yoma 9b, Gitten 57b
288 Zohar Chadash 10
289 Talmud Shabbos 118b
290 Zohar Chai, Genesis 77
291 Sanhedrin 37
292 Mesilat Yesharim 10

"The earth was devastation and desolation, and there was darkness on the face of the deep…"[293] It says in the Midrash that this verse alludes to the kingdoms that took the Jews into exile, causing the light of *HaShem* and that of the *tzaddik* to be hidden. "But the spirit of *HaShem* was hovering over the face of the waters."[294] The spirit of *HaShem* is a spirit of *Moshiach* when he reveals himself to rectify everything. Then how will we be worthy of this? It will be through weeping and mourning over the destruction of the Temple. This is why the spirits of *HaShem* and of *Moshiach* were "hovering over the face of the waters" - the waters of our tears, as it is written, "Pour out your heart like water."[295] "For these, I weep… water comes forth from my eyes, for my comforter is far from me."[296]

If we take our mind and heart back to Syria in the 18th century, we will greatly enjoy the following story: Rabbi Avraham Entabi was the Rav of Aram Tzova, a city in Syria. He told this remarkable story: "In my youth, there was a rabbi of our town called R. Yedidiah ben Dayan, who took upon himself to rise before *chatzos* and walk through the streets together with the *gabbaim*. They would knock at each door of the house of each Jew, telling him to wake up and come to *shul*. *HaShem* was with him, and almost no one let him down. I can honestly tell you that the majority of our community used to get up after *chatzos* and come to *shul*. The townspeople sat in groups. There was a group of young scholars who used to sit learning Gemara; some studied Shulchan Aruch, some Zohar, while others learned *mussar*. Each Thursday night, there were men who spent the whole night in the *shul*. Before the onset of *Shabbos*, Rabbi Yedidiah would bring sufficient oil to light up the entire *shul*, and practically the entire community would come during the night and recite all the Psalms in unison. Afterward, they would recite the Song of Songs. I can testify that all the time they followed this practice, "The children of Israel had light in their dwellings."[297] Throughout those years there were no tragedies, and not a single Jew came to any harm. It was a time period of prosperity and plenty. People were free of worries. Not a single person died before his time. Of that generation, I say, 'and your people are all *tzaddikim*. [298]"[299]

Rabbi Eliyahu Lopian began regularly to recite *Tikkun Chatzos* in his later years. When one of his students asked him why, he responded, "When I leave this world and come before the Heavenly Tribunal, they will question me if I kept the Shulchan Aruch and presumably I'll say I did.

---

293 Genesis 1:2
294 Ibid.
295 Lamentations 2:19
296 Ibid.1: 16
297 Exodus 10,23
298 Isaiah 60,21
299 Korban Isheh, introduction

They're sure to say, let us check, and they'll probably start going through the Shulchan Aruch section by section, law by law. If they catch me on some detail after about two hundred sections, I might be able to come up with an answer. What am I going to say, though, if they catch me on the very first section?"[300]

As Rabbi Lopian has reminded us, the very first section of the Shulchan Aruch speaks about the important practice of *Tikkun Chatzos*. Says the Shulchan Aruch, "It is desirable, if possible, for a person to rise early, to get up at midnight and recite *Tikkun Chatzos*, as it is stated in *Eichah* 2:19, 'Arise, call out at night, at the beginning of the watches.'" Rabbi Yosef Caro goes on to explain how *HaShem* cries out at this time every night over the destruction of the Temple. Therefore, we too should cry out and show *HaShem* how much we want the rebuilding of the Holy Temple.

There are many basic Jewish practices that take priority over this one. Rabbi Yosef Caro, author of the Shulchan Aruch, doesn't say that this practice is something one must follow. Rabbi Shimon Bar Yochai doesn't either, but he says, "Happy will be the portion of the person who rises at that hour to study with zest the holy Torah. *HaShem* will bring to him a thread of grace that will secure him the protection of both the higher and lower angels. As it is said in Psalms, "By the daytime, *HaShem* will command his grace and at night I shall chant his song." Reb Hizkiah said, "Whoever learns Torah at that hour will constantly have a portion in the future world."[301]

King David truly understood the importance of this hour as he spoke of it often in the Psalms: "At midnight I will rise to give thanks to thee."[302] He also said, "Awake my soul, awake lyre and harp, I will awaken the dawn."[303] King Solomon also speaks of this practice and stated, "Arise, cry out in the night at the beginning of the watches, pour out your heart like water in the presence of *HaShem*."[304] We are told, "If the Jewish people were more careful to arise for *chatzos* their enemies would be subdued and would not impose any decrees against them."[305] Rebbe Nachman says, "This *Tikkun*, rectification prayer, has the power of redemption. It sweetens harsh decrees."[306]

The *Tikkun* is broken up into two sections: One is called *Tikkun Rachel* and the other *Tikkun Leah*. *Tikkun Rachel* is said only during days when *Tachanun* is recited. *Tikkun Leah* is recited following *Tikkun Rachel's*

300 R. Moshe Aharon Stern, *Mashgiach*, Kaminetz *Yeshiva*, Jerusalem
301 Zohar 1, 92a
302 Psalms 119,62
303 Psalms 57,9
304 Lamentations 2,19
305 Zohar Chai, Bereshis 77
306 Likutey Moharan 1, 149

recitation on all days and is said alone during days in which *Tikkun Rachel* is not said. The first *Tikkun* speaks primarily of the Temple's destruction and the pains of our nation. *Tikkun Rachel*, on the other hand, focuses more on the love of *HaShem* and drawing close to him.

For some, it may be difficult to institute this prayer into their busy schedule. As difficult as it may be though, the rewards are seven-fold. The holy Baal Shem Tov says, "Convert the nights into days. Sleep a few hours during the day so that you will suffice with but little sleep at night.[307] When rising at midnight, overcome by sleepiness, drive it away by pacing back and forth in the house and chanting hymns with a raised voice. Study a number of [diverse] subjects. Do not concentrate on a single lesson lest it becomes onerous for you. Thus, study many [different] lessons [and that will banish your sleepiness]."[308]

If you have the strength, continue through the night after saying the *Tikkun*, learning Torah or practicing *hisbodidus*. The value of what you can accomplish after *chatzos* with your Torah and prayers is many times greater than at other times. In addition, your level of *yiras Shamayim*[309] increases tremendously. While the world is asleep you have broken your slumber to show *HaShem* your true devotion, and this has a remarkable effect.

The Baal Shem Tov taught his students, "May your fear of Heaven be as great as your fear of flesh and blood."[310] If one's teacher were to come and find him asleep, upon awakening he would tremble in his master's presence. How much more [should one rise with alacrity] when the Creator awakens him from sleep at midnight [to lament the destruction of the Holy Temple and the exile of the Jewish people.]"[311]

Those with an elevated level of mentality do everything they can to arise at *chatzos* and remain awake to learn through the night. When the sun rises from its chambers they run to pray with the early *netz*[312] *minyan*[313]. The Baal Shem Tov said about this, "One should always be sure to arise at midnight, as well as to connect the night to the new day [through one's Divine service]."[314] He also said, *davening* when the sun first rises is like the difference between east and west.

Rav Noson once said, "By getting up at *chatzos*, or at least before

---

307 Sleeping during the day (except on *Shabbos*) is generally disapproved of, especially by the mystics. If it is necessary to enable one to study Torah at night, however, one may "borrow" from day-time to "repay it" in the night
308 Tzava'as Harivash #26-28
309 Fear of Heaven
310 Berachos 28b
311 Kesser Shem Tov 205
312 Morning prayer at sunrise
313 A Minyan is the gathering of 10 men to pray together
314 Tzava'as HaRivash 83

dawn, to join night with day by means of Torah study and *Tefillah*, the night, which is the level of Disorder, becomes included in the level of Order, which is the day.[315]

Once, Rabbi Tzvi Hirsh of Ziditchov and Rabbi Yaakov of Radzimin were in Lublin visiting the great *rebbe*, known as the Seer of Lublin. Before dawn, the holy *rebbe* asked Rabbi Hirsh, "Rabbi Hirshele, has morning come?" He responded, "The daylight has certainly arrived." The *rebbe* then told him to go outside and double check. Rabbi Hirsh went out and realized it was still dark but, realizing the Seer wanted it, agreed with him that it was day. The Seer then commented, "It is still dark, but through the *Tikkun Chatzos* that we did we have clarified the darkness into day."[316]

Someone once heard Rabbi Tzvi Hirsh exclaim, "Many of the great of previous generations who had the Holy Spirit told us to bind together day and night through Torah and prayer."[317]

Each of these devotions, arising for *chatzos* and praying at sunrise, is pious and stands very high. When combined together though, who can imagine the greatness? It certainly is true avodas *HaShem* at the highest level. This should be the goal and dream of every man to perform. Happy are those already holding onto this *madrega*[318]. How pleasant with be their portion in the next world. We as a nation owe them so much gratitude since they are supporting us (explains the Zohar in *Parshas Lech Lecha*). My friends, I only hope that we are supporting them too.

As we have said before, it is the habit of great *tzaddikim* to keep their pious devotions to themselves. The holy Rabbi Naftali of Ropshitz was one who tried to keep his *Tikkun Chatzos* a secret. Once, when he was saying the *Tikkun* prostrated on the floor, he had forgotten to close the door behind him as usual. One of the townspeople entered the room and discovered his *rebbe* in this most unusual position. The *rebbe* immediately jumped up, trying to hide what he was doing. Realizing he was caught, the *Rebbe* said, "Certainly the people of the city don't know the greatness of their rabbi!" The man thought the *rebbe* was saying this out of pride and spoke against him to his fellow townsfolk. This was just as the *rebbe* had intended, hoping he could still keep his devotion a secret.[319]

Rabbi Moshe Leib of Sassov once heard of a poor woman, separated from her husband who was in prison for theft, and she had recently given birth during a frigid winter night. Rabbi Moshe put on the clothing of a gentile peasant, hoping he wouldn't be recognized as he carried on his shoulder firewood he had chopped himself. Arriving at her

---

315 Seder Tikkun Chatzos, p.19 #8
316 Ha-Hozeh mi-Lublin, p. 138
317 Yifrach Bi Yamav Tzaddik, p.39b
318 Level
319 Eser Tzachtzachos, p.88, #22

home, he built a fire and offered her something hot to drink. He then began reciting Tikkun Rochel and Tikkun Leah.[320]

Rabbi Yitzchok Isaac of Ziditchov once remarked that for fifty-four consecutive years he never slept through midnight (except during an emergency), but always arose and said *Tikkun Chatzos*. This meant that he must have begun this practice when he was approximately fourteen years old.[321]

Once after *Shabbos*, Reb Boruch (the landowner) lay down to rest. Suddenly he was startled as he saw a light through his window. Expecting the worst, he got up quickly from his bed to see if there was a fire in one of his rented rooms. As he approached the door of the room lit up, he looked through the keyhole. To his surprise, he saw a poor man sitting on the ground, trembling as he was reciting *Tikkun Chatzos*. He was up to the verse, "Why have you forgotten us for so long? Why have you left us abandoned for such a length of days?" The man's hands were spread and raised. His face shone brightly with a great light and tears were running down his holy cheeks. This man was none other than the Baal Shem Tov.[322]

When Rabbi Chaim of Tzanz returned from the mikvah he used to say *Tikkun Chatzos* with an outpouring of his soul. He said it with such bitter crying that those who were outside his room would themselves break down and begin to wail. After finishing the *Tikkun*, he learned in the Zohar with great *d'vekus* and then repeated Mishnayos from memory, usually from the order of Zeraim.[323]

Every night in Jerusalem, an elite bunch of men would get together in a van and go to the Kotel to recite *Tikkun Chatzos*. When he was a young man, the Nikolsburger Rebbe *shlita* and his followers got together and learned all night. All Thursday and Friday the *rebbe* wouldn't sleep but would continuously learn Torah. Only on *Shabbos* afternoon would he finally replenish his strength with a brief nap. These, my friends, are examples of people who today are supporting the world.

Rabbi Avraham HaLevi, who wrote the Tikkunei Shabbos, lived in Safed in the time of the Arizal. Each night, Rabbi Avraham would arise at *chatzos* and go around the Jewish quarter of the city crying out bitterly, "Jewish brothers, you surely know that the *Shechinah*[324] is in exile because of our numerous sins, and our Holy Temple has been burnt down. Rise up and let us shed tears out to our *HaShem*, who is a loving and compassionate King! Maybe *HaShem* will hear our cries and prayers and have mercy on the remnant of Israel!" Rabbi HaLevi gave no rest to anyone in town, and they

---

320 Menorah ha-Tehorah, p. 51 #10
321 Eser Kedushos, p. 73, #8
322 Sippurei Chassidim, Zevin, vol. 1. #268
323 Sefer Rabbeinu ha-Kodesh miTzanz, p.250
324 Divine Presence

would all arise and go to the *bais medrashim*, where they would recite *Tikkun Chatzos*. Following the recital of the *Tikkun*, everyone studied at his own level or sang songs and prayers until the light of day.

The Arizal praised Rabbi Avraham for his saintliness and said that he was a reincarnation of the prophet Yirmiyahu. Once the Arizal told him, "You should know that your days are coming to a close and the time has come for you to leave the world… unless you accept the following assignment - and if you do, you will remain alive for another twenty-two years. You must depart to *Yerushalayim*[325] and pray at the Western Wall. Pour your heart out, and then you will merit perceiving the *Shechinah*."

The pious Rabbi Avraham locked himself up in his home for three days and nights and sat fasting in sackcloth and ashes. He then went to the Western Wall and poured out his heart in prayer, crying profusely. Suddenly he noticed the form of a woman near the wall. She was swathed in black. Rabbi Avraham was so scared that he fell down on his face weeping and sobbing, "OY! That I have seen you like this! OY! My poor soul!" He cried and cried, pulling at his hair, until ultimately, he fainted and fell into a deep slumber. He dreamed that a holy spirit dressed in beautiful garments came to him and spoke, "Be comforted, my son Avraham, for there is hope for you in the long run: the children will return to their land, for I will free them from their captivity and have pity on them."

After having awoken, Rabbi Avraham journeyed back to Safed. When he came to the Arizal, the latter immediately replied, "I see from your appearance that you had the great honor of glancing at the face of the *Shechinah*. You can now be sure that you will be alive for another twenty-two years." Rabbi Avraham did indeed live for an additional twenty-two years, and he should be a role model for everyone to rise at *chatzos*, or at least before the light of morning, to mourn over the destruction of the Holy Temple. Regardless of whether one says many prayers or just a couple, the main thing is to direct one's heart to Heaven, and then a person will be worthy of seeing the rebuilding of *Yerushalayim, amen.*[326]

It says in the *siddur*[327] of the Shelah, "A man who arises regularly for *Tikkun Chatzos* is a *tzaddik*. A thread of mercy is stretched over him to rescue him from all accusers. He is considered a member of the Court of the King and his *parnasa*[328] is assured."

The night is divided into many watches. During the first part of the evening, the world undergoes its daily judgment and the *kelipos*[329] have access to higher levels, drawing greater nourishment. If this were to be

---

325 Jerusalem
326 Kav HaYashar 93
327 Prayer book
328 Livelihood
329 Spirits of impurity

unchecked, the forces of the Other Side would have too much power and this would adversely affect Creation a great deal. However, the *kelipos* become ensnared by the *mitzvos* and Torah study that we perform, and they lose power. This happens at *chatzos* when the first trace of *chesed's* [330] light starts to manifest in the world. The rectification of *Malchus*[331] then begins, when judgments are stayed and loving-kindness begins to be revealed.[332] Dovid HaMelech once recited, "I will rise up at midnight to give thanks to you for your righteous judgments."[333]

The study of Torah after *chatzos* diminishes the forces of evil.[334] The forces of unholiness are overcome and a person's sins are forgiven. One's intellect and thoughts become purified and one can grasp *HaShem's* unity without confusion. Everyone who wants to come closer to *HaShem* should drive slumber from his eyes at night and devote himself to Torah study and pray in order to triumph over the "husks". This will definitely help him come nearer to *HaShem*.[335]

If the Jewish people would arise at *chatzos*, their enemies would be subdued and would not impress any decrees against them. Our affliction in this bitter exile is caused because of not getting up to study Torah and sing songs of praise after *chatzos*.[336]

Rabbi Chiya taught, "If a person studies the Torah at night, the *Shechinah* resides with that person." This is because it says, "Arise, cry out in the night, at the beginning of the watches; pour out your heart like water before the face of *HaShem*."[337]

"Bless *HaShem*, all of *HaShem's* servants who stand in the house of *HaShem* in the evenings."[338] Rabbi Yochanan remarked, "Those who study Torah at night are considered as if they were engaged in the Temple service."[339]

"Just as the Exodus from Egypt started at *chatzos*, so too the final redemption will begin at *chatzos*. It will come about in the merit of those who arise for *chatzos*."[340]

In Kedushas Levi it says, "When a person has holy thoughts and mourns over Jerusalem, his thoughts and very essence are imbued with holiness. Through this practice, even at present, one can see and experience

---

330 One of the Sefiros/literal translation loving kindness
331 One of the Sefiros/literal translation Kingship
332 Zohar 1, 92b
333 Psalms 119:62
334 Zohar 1,248
335 Reishis Chockmah, Sha'ar HaKedushah 7
336 Zohar Chai, Bereshis 77
337 Talmud Tamid 32b
338 Psalms 134:1
339 Menachos 110a
340 Likutey Halakhos, Hashkamas HaBoker 1:15

something of the joy of Jerusalem as it will be in the time to come."

The Iyun Yaakov teaches that Torah study at night is called true Torah because his meritorious deed is hidden from others. This is in contrast with Torah study done during the day when his deed (though it may not be his motive) is seen and wins him recognition. Studying at night is, therefore, intrinsic study, which can be considered *lishma*[341].[342]

Torah study during the night is very beneficial because of the modesty it instills. Our rabbis have suggested to us that it is better to study with ulterior motives (studying solely for fame, wealth, etc.) than not at all. This is because the study that is *shelo lishma*[343] leads to study done *lishma*.[344] Though study *shelo lishma* is not without value, since it is a commandment for a man to learn Torah, it doesn't reach the true potential for elevating the *Malchus* as it should. Torah study at night, more specifically Torah *she ba'al peh*[345], brings loving kindness upon a person and, not only that but has the ability to transform one's study for personal gain into studying *lishmah*.[346] To understand this idea more, you can look at Likutey Moharan Chapter 3.

The Netziv teaches us that, during the time of the *Bais Hamikdash*, if a person wanted to find favor in *HaShem's* eyes he would take a sacrifice to the *kohen hagadol* as an offering to *HaShem*. This brought Divine sustenance to the person who brought the sacrifice and to the entire world. After the *Beis Hamikdash* was destroyed, the only way that a person can attain Divine sustenance is to arise and study at night. The Talmud says, "One who learns Torah at night is graced with the presence of the *Shechinah*[347], as the verse states, 'Arise and study at night in the presence of *HaShem.*'"

In the time of exile, the righteous are no longer supported by the sacrifices of the *kohanim*. *Chazal* teaches us that prayer has taken the place of sacrifices. Prayer can reach many elevated levels, but it reaches exceptional heights when Torah learning follows it. This is especially true during *chatzos*, the time of favor for the entire world. The righteous used to concern themselves only with spiritual matters in the time of the Temple. Now that she is destroyed, they have additional responsibilities that the *Kohanim* can no longer shoulder. They have to support the world and bring blessings down through their prayers, as the Talmud teaches, "Just as the *Kohanim* were obligated to present sacrifices to draw forth Divine bounty and win acceptance for the prayers and requests of the people, so too scholars are obligated to pray on behalf of Israel."[348]

---

341 For the sake of Heaven
342 Talmud Chagigah
343 Not for the sake of Heaven
344 Pesachim 50b
345 Oral Torah, (the written Torah corresponds to Z'er Anpin and the oral Torah Malchus)
346 Parparos LeChokhmah
347 Tamid, end of fourth perek
348 Netziv, Shir Hashirim

"If the Temple is not built in one's days, it is as if it was destroyed in our lifetime.[349] There is a responsibility that each of us has to care and mourn over the Temple and Jerusalem. It is a responsibility that we should no longer ignore. We don't even know our own loss, as we are so removed from holiness. If we were to comprehend our loss completely, we could no longer enjoy life in this world. The physicality and honor we each strive for are so wasteful. Our whole lives and entire being should be devoted only to bring one another back to *HaShem*, to do *chesed* and learn Torah. How can we not feel the pangs of *Moshiach* and not hear the wailing from the *Kotel*? The message should be clear; the *Shechinah* is in exile. We are in exile. Let's do our part to end this pain in all the worlds. There is a wailing from one end of the world to the other. In the heavens, our tears are counted. No tear goes to waste; each tear is collected in Heaven. Let our hearts be open to feel the needs of our fellow and let us be sensitive to the needs of the *Shechinah*. We can make a difference and bring this exile to a close. Let us realize that it all starts with us.

The Baal HaTanya advises, "The time for *teshuvah tata'a*[350], is designated at *Tikkun Chatzos*. Whoever cannot do this nightly should maintain an absolute minimum of once every week, before the *Shabbos*, Thursday night."[351] Reb Shneur Zalman also says that a person should realize that through his sins he continues the exile of the *Shechinah*.[352] Rebbe Nachman says something similar: "Perhaps in a previous incarnation, we actually did cause the destruction of the Temple. Therefore, it is fitting that each of us makes certain that at least we are not responsible for the delay in rebuilding it. Thus, we must make the effort to get up for *chatzos* and mourn the destruction of the Temple. *HaShem* has promised to reward all those who mourn by allowing them to witness the rebuilding of the Temple and Jerusalem.[353] Rebbe Nachman also compares the Holy Temple to our own *da'as*[354]. When someone's mind, *da'as*, is pure, it is as if the Temple were built. However, when man's mind is blemished, this indicates the destruction of the Holy Temple.[355]

Close to two hundred years ago, there lived a *tzaddik*, Rabbi Yitzchak Isaac Eichenstein of Safrin *zt"l* and his pious wife Hinda *zt"l*. Together they raised five sons, all of whom were great <u>Torah</u> giants in their generation. Rabbi Tzvi Hirsch of Zidichov *zt"l* was the best-known and greatest.

---

349 Yerushalmi, Yoma 1:1
350 To arouse divine compassion
351 Igeres Hateshuvah, chapt.10
352 Tanya Ig-Hateshuvah ch.7
353 Likutey Moharan II, 67
354 Knowledge
355 Likutey Moharan II, 67

Rebbetzin Hinda was known for her gentle heart and kind deeds. She had the custom to rise every night at *chatzos*. She would sit alone on the ground and quietly recite the *Tikkun* with streams of tears from her eyes. Having begotten children, she still remained strong in her devotion of rising every night and saying *Tikkun Chatzos*. Not only was she devoted to arising herself, but she would also wake her sons with her, even when they were only infants, and sit them beside her on the ground. The children would also cry with her (though it might have been for other reasons as well). The holy *rebbetzin* explained that if she wanted to teach her children that a Jew must arise at *chatzos*, she had better get them used to it right away. If she "pampered" them by letting them sleep through the night, who knows if in future years they would be able to break the habit.

Though it might appear excessive, her logic apparently bore fruits. In later years, she used to say that she had no fear of the Heavenly Court that would judge her after death. "Even if I personally am not worthy of a place in *Gan-Eden*, they will have to grant it to me because of my five pious sons!" She paraphrased the verse, "I will ascend *bamesilah* (on the straight path)."[356] Each of these letters *bamesilah*, she said, was an acronym for the names of her five sons: Berish, Moshe, Sender, Lipa and Hershel.

Rabbi Elijah deVidas said, "It seems to me that this practice is a basic pillar for all the service of *HaShem*. It is also not by accident that the service at midnight is emphasized so much throughout the Zohar, innumerable times, more so than all the other *mitzvos*."[357] Rebbe Nachman once remarked, "A Jew's main devotion is to rise at midnight".[358] We have spoken here mostly about the importance of learning and the recital of the *tikkun* at this hour but let us not forget the importance of *hisbodidus*[359]. There is no greater time for *hisbodidus* than from midnight until daylight when the entire world is sleeping. This is the time when you can make accounts with your Creator and search your ways.[360]

Rabbi Tzvi Hirsh of Ziditchov said on this matter, "I have received a tradition from our rabbis that *Tikkun Chatzos* arouses in Heaven a special time of Divine favor when a person's sins are forgiven. My brothers, there is no superior time for *hisbodidus* and for separation from worldly matters, when the worldly thoughts will not disturb you, then at *chatzos*. This is the time to arouse yourself to stand up and pray for the welfare of your despondent soul, which through her sins has become distant from the source of pure living waters and coarsened through involvement with the body, which has its root in the lowly dust.

---

356 Numbers 20:19
357 Totzaos Chayim p.23
358 Sichos Haran, #301
359 See chapter Hisbodidus
360 Seder Tikkun Chatzos, p.12

At this hour you should search well to uncover those things you have done that are worthy of shame, and you should talk from your heart to *HaShem*, like a servant before his Master... with soft-spoken words, humbling yourself, and with verses about *HaShem's* mercy, to converse like a son before his father. All that he says in prayer should be in his native language that he speaks and understands so that he can pour out his soul without difficulty and can express fully the pain of his heart over his sins and transgressions. He should ask for pardon and forgiveness and beg *HaShem* Who made him and formed him that He come and help to bring us close to His service so that we will fear Him with all our hearts. This *teshuvah* is the entire purpose of getting up at midnight. When you consider all this before going to bed, pray that from heaven they will wake you at midnight [that you will be successful waking up then], and then you will go to sleep without uncertainties and be at peace!"[361]

There are those who say that laws of Judaism and customs of the past don't apply in our modern day and age. What will these people answer when they are brought before the *bais din shel maala?*[362] We still remain, as does the *Shechinah*, in exile! *HaShem* still calls out, "Woe to my children who have been exiled." The pains of our exile have if anything increased over the years. In our generation when so many have forgotten their identity it is even more imperative than ever to arise for *chatzos*. We need to show *HaShem* that we care, and we still mourn the loss of our Temple. It is not enough to learn Torah and yet ignore entirely the most precious hours of the day. "Awake, my soul, awake," said Dovid as he stirred himself out of bed at this hour, not forgetting about the *Shechinah*. Each night he would compose Psalms to *HaShem* and try to fix the world. Not only have we the ability to fix our own *neshamos* by saying *Tikkun Chatzos* but also the entire world, just like Dovid HaMelech. Shall we sleep through these precious hours of the night? If so, who will it be to bring the final redemption if not us?

---

361 DhTvhY, Hashkamas ha-Boker, #22
362 The Heavenly Court

TEFILAH TIKKUN CHATZOS

Thank You, HaShem for giving us the Torah and commandments. How do I begin to speak to You about how much we need the Temple to be rebuilt in this generation? There is so much bloodshed, Anti-Semitism, immorality, crime, hunger, loneliness, and sadness in the world. My self-confidence is shattered just thinking about how much has to be done to bring perfection to a world so full of confusion. I have learned that there is a special prayer, unlike any other, that can help bring an end for all of us to this long and bitter exile. Unfortunately, this is a difficult devotion to practice successfully, as it entails waking up in the middle of the night when I am already tired out from my work and studies. HaShem, I understand how important this practice is and I want to incorporate it into my life as the great tzaddikim of old used to do, but I need a full yeshua[363] in order to do so. I need help to control my Yetzer Hara[364], which does not want to let me rise at this precious hour of avodas HaShem. Also, I need support from my family such that they too understand the importance of this avodah.

When I'm successful in rising at this hour, please help me to use my time wisely by saying the Tikkun Chatzos prayer, repenting, doing hisbodidus and learning Torah. Help me please, HaShem, to remain awake often from chatzos until the morning sunrise, learning Torah with tremendous enthusiasm. By my practice, let the evil in the world lose strength and be diminished.

Saying the Tikkun is good, HaShem, but to say it with all my heart, how precious it will be in your eyes. Help me to understand a little bit of our true loss at this hour and truly feel our present exile. Let the remembrance of the Bais Hamikdash's destruction be real in my heart. Help me feel shame over my sins, my ancestors' and the sins of our nation. May my prayers at this hour be so heartfelt that my eyes come to tears! After having expressed and felt the destruction of our Temple, please help me return to joy at the thought of the imminent redemption, as otherwise, my heart would not be able to contain its anguish.

HaShem, please help me to not let this propitious hour slip by. Dovid HaMelech never slept past this hour as he took control over his time and life. I want to do the same and serve you righteously; never forgetting that there is a Shechinah in exile waiting for me to bring her home. Help me HaShem to know and never forget that I too can make a difference by rising for chatzos. Thank You, HaShem for opening the gates to my prayers as you have done so often. There may be millions of prayers entering the gates of heaven, but nonetheless, you don't turn my words away but rather welcome them.

---

363 Salvation
364 Evil inclination

CHAPTER 8: TEFILLAH, PRAYER & SPEECH

"Let Him kiss me with the kisses of His mouth." (Song of Songs 1:2)

Most of us are pretty confident that we know how to pray to *HaShem*. There are those of us who pray quickly, skipping over many words in the process, and there are those who are more meticulous, taking their time. Some of us leave overconfident, thinking our prayers have opened up the Heavens while really, they have lacked true heartfelt devotion. So, instead of piercing through the gates as they think, their prayers have headed downwards. Some are aware of their passiveness, realizing they lack the knowledge how really come close to *HaShem* through prayer.

Let us be honest and admit we have very little idea why the Great Assembly laid out the *siddur*[365] the way they did. We never attended the board meetings they had and, even if we did, we still wouldn't have a clue. The remarkable understanding of our sages, of *p'sukim* and Talmud, are beyond our wildest imagination. They wove together letters and words like a tailor preparing a beautiful garment for a king. If they saw us now flying through the prayer service so haphazardly, what would they think?

With this in mind, the best way to approach the *siddur* would be to understand the purpose and meaning of prayer as *HaShem* intended it. Then it also makes sense to try and learn how the greatest and simplest Jews used the prayer service as a guide to drawing closer to *HaShem*. Only then can we start to imagine the thought process behind the great Assembly in uniting the prayer service.

Since the beginning of man's creation, he has been given the opportunity and privilege to approach his Creator via speech. We have so much to be thankful for just being privileged to speak to the King of Kings,

---

365 Prayer book

Master of the World. How many of us get to speak to people of notable stature in our lifetime? They are too busy, and they don't have time for everyone, especially the common folk. When was the last time you spoke to the President? It is difficult enough just to reach your best friend on the phone in the middle of the day! When *HaShem* created man, he desired that there be constant feedback between Him and His creations. Not only does he expect us to constantly praise Him, but also to ask Him for all of our physical and spiritual needs, constantly. There is no human or terrestrial being that can come even close to being there for us as our Creator, Blessed Be He. When we need something, He is the only one we can truly count on to be there for us.

There is a story in the Talmud, in which a king provides his children their monetary allowances each day. Even though the king could have given their allowances in a lump sum once or twice a year, he knew his approach would ensure that he saw his children on a daily basis.[366]

It is not that *HaShem* needs our prayers or regular contact; rather, He wants us close because He loves us. *HaShem* does not want us to just list our requests; this is not the true inner purpose of prayer. "Prayer is an introspective procedure, a helpful, refining process of discovering what one is, what he should be, and how to achieve a transformation of self. In reality, the commandment to pray is considered by the Torah as a service of the heart, not of the mouth[367]."[368]

"To love the *HaShem*, your *HaShem* and to serve Him with all your heart."[369] The terminology 'with your heart' means prayer. Pray with love and *HaShem* will love your supplications, as Reb Zeira explained: a man may have a loving friend, but as soon as he asks a favor of him or needs his help, the man becomes his enemy and rebuffs him. But *HaShem* loves a man better the more he begs, invokes and prays. He even asks man to pray to Him, as it is said, "Call unto Me and I will answer you."[370]

Let us review for a few moments the abilities we have been given to communicate; this is so vital to our service of *HaShem*. We can write, use hand signals and physical gestures, type and of course speak. All these forms are good, but nothing can compare to our ability to talk. The tongue is the pen of a person's heart.[371] It is what differentiates us from other life forms and it gives our life meaning.

It is remarkable how, by just listening to people around him, a child learns how to speak mostly on his own. Given this ability, he then learns

---

366 Talmud Yoma 76a

367 Taanis 2a

368 Artscroll Siddur, Introduction

369 Devarim 6:5

370 Shochar Tov 4

371 Chovos Halevavos

how to communicate his needs and yearnings to his parents. We need to learn how to communicate also to our Creator, Blessed Be He, through prayer.

The Koznitzer Maggid said, "We are bits of dust, full of sin and evil. Even so, we are worthy of speaking and petitioning before the King of Glory, the Creator of all, of whom it is said, 'No thought can grasp Him at all.'" [372] We can also call *HaShem*, "YOU" as if we were talking to another person standing in front of us. This is certainly a great expression of *HaShem*'s love. It is the miracle of *HaShem*'s love and mercy toward all creatures. [373]

It is written, "Fear not, O worm Jacob." [374] Why is Israel likened to a worm? A worm is a soft creature; it can fell the mightiest cedars, but only with its mouth. Similarly, Israel can make use of prayer. [375]

It is important to understand the strength we have in our tongues. Putting prayer aside for a moment, let us explore this strength in a general sense. Just by speaking we have the ability to save or destroy another person. Shlomo HaMelech said, "Life and death are in the power of the tongue." [376] A *shochet* [377] was suspended on suspicion that he had used a dented knife. Rabbi Yisrael Salanter having been approached about this replied, "Who knows how many dents were in the knife that slaughtered the *shochet*?"

Rabbi Yisrael Meir Kagan, the author of Chofetz Chayim, spells out thirty-one *mitzvos* that are desecrated when one speaks or listens to *loshon hara* [378]. [379] With ten trials were our forefathers tried and in all of them, their fate was not sealed except for the sin of gossip. [380] After telling over a nice piece of *loshon hara*, how are we able then to pray using the same tongue? It is important to understand, "There is a time for silence and a time for speaking." [381]

The Chofetz Chaim used to say that some people were mistaken about his book on *loshon hara*. "It's not a book against speaking. On the contrary, the book gives a person permission to speak. But before you know the laws, how can you speak? You might be violating a Torah prohibition. Once you have studied the laws, you know what is permissible to say." [382] Only then can you really begin to talk and make use of this

---

372 Tikuney Zohar 17a
373 Avodath Yisroel, Lekh Lekha 6a
374 Isaiah 41:14
375 Midrash Tanchuma, BeShalach 9
376 Mishlei 18:21
377 Ritual slaughterer
378 Evil talk
379 Sefer Shemiras Halashon
380 Avos de R' Noson 9
381 Ecclesiastes

precious tool.

On no account let anything be uttered by you unless you know that it is the will of *HaShem* that you say it.[383] Rabbi Yossi Ber of Brisk always had a snuffbox on his table. When he was about to converse with someone, he would begin by opening it up, glance in it, and then he would begin the discussion. Someone close to him could not overcome his curiosity, and took a look inside: he found carved the abbreviation W.K.H.M.A.T.K.H.F.T. Not understanding what this meant, he asked the rabbi, who told him: "It is from the verse of scripture, 'Whoso keeps his mouth and tongue, keeps himself from trouble.'"[384][385]

We are taught, "The mundane speech of scholars requires study."[386] Rabbi Moshe of Dolina said, "I heard the following explanation from the holy lips of the Baal Shem Tov. The main perfection of the righteous is that their attachment to *HaShem* does not cease, even for an instant. The same is true of all their speech. Even when they must speak to people about worldly things, they seek to do it in a way that their attachment to *HaShem* is not broken off. Since such a person remains attached to *HaShem* even in his mundane speech, such words require study."[387]

The tone in which one speaks is very important. The Ramban wrote to his son: "One should always speak gently and calmly to everyone. This will prevent a person from anger, which is a serious character flaw that causes one to sin."[388] When speaking to me the Hornosteipel Rebbe, Rabbi Shalom Friedman, would talk in a sweet whisper, so as to continue his attachment with the *Shechinah*. When he had to tell me, I was doing something wrong, he spoke so softly that he only drew me closer. If it was something difficult for me to hear, it didn't matter as it was spoken to me in a gentle tone. This is the way we all should talk. If we did, it would remove anger from our hearts entirely. When a person is angry, people don't want to associate with him and, to the same degree, the *Shechinah*[389] turns aside. This is because the *Shechinah* attaches itself to our mouth.

We can also affect life in the spiritual worlds through our mouths. The Vilna Gaon once told, "Just as rain and all existence on earth are dependent on the evaporation of water, so are all the heavenly activities that affect life on earth dependent upon human speech."

It is also important to always think before one speaks. A person should weigh his words as if his entire being is on a balance beam and can

---

382 Rabbi Shmuel Pliskin in Der Chofetz Chaim, p.71
383 Derech Chayim, 2-17
384 Proverbs 21:23
385 Midor Dor, Vol. 2, #1619
386 Succah 21b
387 Rabbi Moshe of Dolina, Divrey Moshe, VaYera, Sefer Baal Shem Tov, Berashith 107
388 Ramban's Letter to his son
389 Divine Presence

tip over to the good or bad side by one small mistake. Using such caution brings one to a fear of *HaShem* that enables one to use his speech like an arrow in the hands of a marksman. Those who are wise will understand this.

When your words are used to flying out of your mouth without prior thought and reason, you can't possibly apply yourself properly when it comes time to pray. A person, who prays without knowing what he prays, does not really pray.[390] One must concentrate his whole heart on the prayers. It is no good if the heart is far from the words the mouth is speaking. Therefore, one must listen carefully to what he is saying.[391] A person should attain a level in prayer where there is only *HaShem* and himself.[392]

Rabbi Elimelech suggested, "Pray with all your strength. Use your voice to arouse your feelings and connect your thoughts to your words. Face the wall, look into the *siddur* morning and evening, and do not look to the side from the commencement of the service until the end. When the reader repeats the *Amidah*, look into the *siddur* and answer *amen* to each blessing with all your strength." [393]

When he prayed with the congregants, Rabbi Akiva's concentration in prayer was exceptional. But when he prayed by himself it was with such fervor that a man could leave him in one corner and find him later in another.[394] So great was his concentration that he was no longer aware of his physical surroundings.

In a similar story, "When the Mitteler Rebbe would say *tehillim* his *yarmulke* would be drenched through and through!"[395]

I once had an opportunity to be with the Tush Rebbe of Montreal zt"l during a private *minyan* for his closest students. I saw that when the *rebbe davened* he was literally on fire. I glanced down at his feet while studying his outward motions. I noticed that even his little toes were shaking when he said *HaShem's* holy Name. The next time he said *HaShem's* name, even I was filled with fear of Heaven. So great was his *kavanah* that it spread to others in the room.

When I visit the holy Nikesberger Rebbe, I am eager to hear every word he recites in prayer. When he opens his lips to pray, I feel the truth of the Torah and all I know thereafter is that I want to come close to *HaShem*.

It is understandable that a great Rabbi should pray with a lot of kavanah, but what about the common Jew? It is the simple Jew's prayer that

390 Maimon b.Yoseph
391 Likutey Etzos, tefillah #45
392 Likutey Maharan II, 103
393 Tzetel Katan 11
394 Berachos 31a
395 From My Father's Shabbos Table p.144

HaShem truly desires. A simple word recited with all one's heart, even without understanding, can pierce the gates of heaven like a rocket ship. Chazal teach us that a simple Jew's prayers can reach levels in Heaven that even tzaddikim may not reach.

Not long ago in Russia, a young lady wanted to pray to *HaShem* on *Yom Kippur*. The communists who employed her would never understand her request for a day off from work. It meant so much to her to pray on the holy day that she did the craziest thing: She went to the dentist complaining of a pain in her tooth. The doctor felt the tooth and could not find anything wrong with it. She screamed and shouted as he touched it until finally, he asked her, would you like me to just pull it? She said yes and showed the doctor's note to her employers, who gladly told her to stay home a day and recover from the extraction. That *Yom Kippur,* the young lady's prayers opened the heavens and went straight through.[396]She was just a normal person like you and me but her sincerity in prayer is beyond our grasp.

Having just returned from a trip to *Eretz Yisrael,* a *chassid* of the Tzemach Tzedek told his rabbi that he was disappointed, having expected to find many people of greater spirituality there. The Tzemach Tzedek asked, "What makes you assume you are a maven on people of spirituality?" His rabbi continued with the following story: "In *Eretz Yisrael* there lived in the country a farmer who had no access to a rabbi. He was very devout, but completely ignorant when it came to learning Torah, so much so that he was unable to read the calendar. Therefore, each month he would make a trip into the city and the *rabbi* would write out for him a detailed sheet of instructions as to what prayers he should say each day of the upcoming month. One year the *rabbi* called for a day of public fasting and prayers to end the terrible drought they were experiencing. It just so happened that on the day of the fast the farmer happened to need something in town. He was surprised to hear that the *rabbi* had called for a public fast since he hadn't informed him during his prior trip to the city. The *rabbi* explained that this was not a regular fast day and he had no advanced knowledge of its coming. "There has been no rain, and this is a very serious matter that requires us to fast," the *rabbi* explained.

The man seemed puzzled, "Why do you have to fast if there is no rain?" he asked. If I need rain for my farm, I just go out and look towards the sky then say, 'Father, I need rain,' and it commences to rain."

The *rabbi* followed him as he went outdoors, lifted his eyes to the sky, and said in a tearful tone, "Father, your children are in need of rain!" Moments later, clouds appeared, and the needed rainfall began. "Now," the Tzemach Tzedek said, "Do you think you can tell who a spiritual person is?"[397]

396 Glimpses of Greatness p.37
397 Not Just Stories p. 175

I heard from my *rebbe* [the Baal Shem Tov] that even after Rabbi Nehunia ben Hakaneh knew all the [kabalistic] meditations connected with prayer, he would still pray like a small child.[398]

It is important to not overcomplicate one's prayers. Just by forcing yourself to concentrate on the simple meaning of the words, you can reach great levels of *kavanah*. Rebbe Nachman says, "The essence of prayer entails straightforward, simple understanding of the words."[399] When the *rebbe* was deathly ill, he asked his grandson, Yisrael, to pray for him. "*HaShem, HaShem!*" Little Yisrael called out, "let my grandfather be well!" Those nearby smiled when hearing his cute response. To their surprise, the *rebbe* responded, "This is how you are supposed to pray, with simplicity. What other way is there?[400]

An individual should pray with all his might and strength. If a person were to concentrate just on his prayers, the words themselves would give him the energy to pray with all his might."[401]

Reb Noson of Nemerov explains, "Pour out your heart before *HaShem…*"[402] If you can't pray suitably, pour your heart out, even without *kavanah*, just as water might pour out accidentally.[403] Eventually, your heart will open in the right way and you will start praying in the appropriate way with *kavanah*.

After completing one's prayers, a person should ask himself, did I say one word with all my heart? Do you know how great a feeling it is to say one-word *b'emes* [with truth]? There is an elderly gentleman in our community, Rabbi Potoki, who understands the meaning of praying with all his heart. He is a survivor of the gas chambers in Auschwitz. When he prays, he has his mind and heart on the six million Jews who passed on in the Holocaust. The other week, I mentioned to him that when he says *Kaddish*, all six million get an *aliyah*[404]. He responded, "I try, I really try." A teardrop fell from his eye. I found that, even when Rabbi Potoki spoke of normal everyday conversations, he didn't forget the six million. He once said to me, "Moshe, when I talk, people don't realize I really mean what I say with all my heart." He once told me that, when the war first broke out, his *rebbe* told the disciples, stop learning. You can't learn Talmud when there is a knife to your back. For the next eight weeks, they were to memorize the entire Sefer Tehillim as he instructed them. Until his last day, Rabbi Potoki said all of Tehillim twice daily, sometimes still by heart, and

398 Ketonet Passim, p. 43b, Sefer Baal Shem Tov, Noah 134
399 Likutey Maharan II, 120
400 Tzaddik #439
401 *Rebbe* Nachman's Wisdom 66
402 Lamentations 2:19
403 Likutey Halachos, Minchah 7:44.
404 Elevation

recited it with all his devotion!

After prayers one day, Rabbi Levi Yitzchak of Berdichev went over to one of the congregants and wished him a very warm *shalom alechem*! Startled, the man replied, "But I've been here the whole time." The *rabbi* responded, "But during the prayers, your mind wandered to Warsaw where you were pondering about your business. Now that your prayers are completed, you have returned here to Berdichev! So, it was only warranted that I greet you on your safe return."

One thing we lack, especially in our generation, is the ability to focus. This is because we are so impatient and used to the animated distractions of computers and movies. In order to pray to *HaShem*, you must have some strategy how to deal with your wandering mind. An important approach is to attach your thoughts to the holiness of the words and the Hebrew alphabet. Every word is a complete concept and therefore you must place all your strength into it. If you do not, it remains incomplete.[405] Have respect not only for the meaning of the words but also for the letters of the words themselves. Each letter is an entire world just waiting to be created from your lips.

Our main link to *HaShem* is through words - words of Torah and prayer. Every single letter [in these words] has an inner spiritual essence. You must fasten your thought and innermost being to this essence. This is the mystery of, "Let Him kiss me with the kisses of His mouth"[406] - the attachment of spirit to spirit.[407] It is also the mystery of, "If you lie between the lips."[408] When you draw out a word and do not want to let it go, then you are in such a state of attachment.[409] You are attached to *HaShem* with the inner essence of your soul root.

Rabbi Moshe of Kobrin said, "When someone says the word *baruch*[410] he should say it with all his energy until he does not even have energy left to say the next word, *ata*[411]. The Holy One, blessed be He, will then give him new energy to say *ata*. So, should it be for each and every word, that in saying it he gives up all his energy [to *HaShem*], and *HaShem* will bestow on him new energy to say the next word.[412] This is the mystery of drawing out the letters and words so that you come to their root. Through practicing this method, you will come to tremendous concentration in prayer.

Place each of your thoughts into the power of your words, until you see the light of the words. You will then be able to see how one-word

---

405 Likutim Yakarim 2, Tzavaas HaRivash 34
406 Song of Songs 1:2
407 Zohar 2:254a, 2:266b. See Berachos 8a
408 Psalms 68:14
409 Keter Shem Tov #44
410 Blessed
411 Are you
412 Mazkeret Shem ha-Gedolim, p. 192

shines into another, and how many lights are brought forth in their midst. This is the meaning of the verse, "Light is sown for the righteous, and joy to the upright at heart." (Psalms, 97:11) The lights in the letters are *HaShem's* chambers, into which He transmits His emanations.[413]

When we go to shul, it is difficult to just to look in the *siddur* for a long time and not look around at the people around us. It is human nature, but it is something we must fight and overcome. If we are not looking at the words in the *siddur*, our eyes belong closed in trying to grasp a spiritual state of mind. Allowing our minds to wander will certainly not help us to concentrate.

Talking during prayers not only violates the Shulchan Aruch but is also disrespectful to those around us who are trying so hard to concentrate. It is forbidden even to speak words of Torah in the middle of prayers, let alone talk of worldly matters. Speaking in a low voice is not excusable and usually still affects others. I know it is a long service and it is difficult to be still the entire duration, but many people don't go to shul to *daven* as they suffer so much discomfort from others talking. A shul is a place to increase one's fear of Heaven; you wouldn't dare stand in the king's office and talk to someone else, so why should you do so in *HaShem's* house of prayer!

Our *davening* should be strictly for *HaShem* and not show off our *kavanah* to our neighbors. At the same time though, we should not feel embarrassed to properly arouse ourselves towards *kavanah* during prayers. After all, that is the reason we are here and maybe the person we are afraid will hear us could actually be inspired by our *kavanah*.

When you first begin to pray, it is important to wake up your physical body with sounds and movements. Therefore, at the outset, you should arouse your body with all your might. Only then will the power of your soul shine for you. The Zohar thus teaches, "If a fire does not burn intensely, tap the wood, and it blazes forth. To the same effect, if the light of the soul does not burn brightly, tap the body, so the light of the soul should blaze forth."[414] When Rabbi Mordechai of Lechovitz prayed, he roared like a lion until the hearts of all who heard him would shatter and melt like water.[415] Others would make use of rocking and sway their bodies.

Once you have succeeded in lighting your soul, your body should become for you less and less significant. In fact, your goal should be to freeze in place, screaming in a whisper, praying with your soul alone. This is not always an easy level to reach but it is within our capabilities.

When a person does this successfully he can worship in thought alone, without moving any part of his body. When a person links to *HaShem* in the Supernal Universe, he must be careful not to allow his body to move,

---

413 Magid Devarav LeYaakov (Jerusalem, 1971) #52
414 Zohar 3:168a
415 Mazkeret Shem ha-Gedolim, p. 119, 103

since this will spoil his attachment.[416]

Accustom yourself to pray and recite the Psalms in a very low voice. Scream quietly, reciting the words with all your strength. This is the significance of the verse, "All my bones shall say [HaShem, who is like You]."[417] A scream that results from total attachment [to HaShem] is absolutely silent.[418]If you ever see a great tzaddik say a blessing, you will notice how his voice seems to emanate from deep in his throat. This is because he has reached such total attachment to HaShem that all his body is calling out in prayer.

Rebbe Nachman says "A Jew's main attachment to HaShem is through prayer."[419] Therefore, we must never give up trying to pray with all our strength. I am unsure if it is because of laziness that we don't apply ourselves to our prayers, or a tendency to give up too easily. If only we realized how simple true prayer is and just wholeheartedly prayed with all our heart.

A man approached Rebbe Nachman [telling him his great difficulty speaking to HaShem in prayer], asking for advice. In response, the rebbe shared with him the following parable: Once a great general girded himself for battle and had to surmount a mighty wall. When he came to the gate he found it blocked with a spider web. Could you envision anything more foolish than returning in defeat because a spider web is blocking your path? This parable teaches us a crucial lesson. You may find it difficult to speak before HaShem. This is mere foolishness. It is nothing more than laziness and a lack of virtuous boldness.[420] Here you are ready to use your words [of prayer] to overcome the great battle of evil within you. You are right on the verge of victory and about to break down walls with your words. The gates are ready to fly open any second. Should you then hold back because of mere bashfulness? Should you remain silent because of a minor barrier like this? You are about to break down a mighty wall. Will you be discouraged and turn away because of a spider web?[421]

The Talmud talks about, "things that stand in the highest places of the universe and are taken lightly by people."[422] The Baal Shem Tov explained that the effects of prayer are often manifest in the "highest places of the universe," and not in the physical world. It is for this reason that prayer is taken lightly by people, since they assume that their prayer is in vain. The truth, however, is that all prayer has an effect.[423]

---

416 Likutey Yekarim 33
417 Psalms 35:10
418 Likutey Yekarim 6, Keter Shem Tov 166. cf. Sichos HaRan 16
419 Likutey Maharan II,84
420 Azuth DeKedushah. See Betza 25b, Avos 5:20, Orach Chaim 1:1 in Hagah; Likutey Maharan 22:4, 147, 271
421 Sichos HaRan 232
422 Berachos 6b

There are a couple of prerequisites for prayer to be acceptable. The first is that one's prayer should not be a burden and the second is that the prayer should be pure.[424] The person who is persistent in knocking will succeed in entering.[425]

Rebbe Nachman frequently encouraged people to meditate and converse with *HaShem*. He taught, "Even if many days and years pass and it seems that you have accomplished nothing with your words, do not give up. Each word makes an impact."

It is written, "Water wears away stone."[426] It may appear that water dripping on a stone cannot make any impression. Nevertheless, after many years, it can, in fact, make a hole in the stone. We can actually see this.[427] Your heart may be similar to stone. It may seem that your words of prayer make no impression on it at all. Still, as the days and years pass, your heart of stone will also be penetrated.[428]

There are periods when you feel that you cannot pray. During these days, do not give up trying. Instead, reinforce yourself all the more, and stir up your awe of *HaShem*. This is similar to a king in battle, who must disguise himself [so as not to be recognized by the enemy]. Those who are wise are able to distinguish the king by his motions. Individuals who are less wise can still recognize the king since numerous guards constantly surround him. The same holds true when you cannot pray with devotion. You should know that the king is nearby, and you are encountering his guards. The only reason you are not able to come close to the King is the abundant protection surrounding Him. You must, therefore, fortify yourself with reverence, great strength, and intensity in order [to break through this barrier] and come close to *HaShem*. If you are successful, you will then be able to pray with the utmost possible feeling.[429]

One way to increase your concentration during prayer is to clap your hands.[430] By doing this, Rebbe Nachman says, "The air of the place where a man of Israel prays is purified and the air of holiness is drawn there, as if in the Land of Israel itself. And so, when you pray, it is the air of the Land of Israel, which is a remedy for foreign thoughts in prayer."[431]

The secret ingredient in the *ketores*, the spices offered to *HaShem* in the Temple every morning and afternoon, was the *malas ashan*, and it was

---

423 Toldos Yaakov Yosef, Shlach, p.134b, Keter Shem Tov #138
424 The Vilna Goan
425 Moshe Ibn Ezra
426 Job 14:10
427 Avos Rabbi Nasan 6:2
428 Sichos HaRan 234
429 Likutim Yakarim #63, Tzavaas HaRivash #72
430 In places where this is not a common practice, clapping should be done in a way not to disturb another from concentration
431 Likutey Aytzos, Tefillah, #41

kept private in one family. The *malas ashan* allowed the smoke from the offering to go straight up to Heaven in a perfect vertical line and made the offering pleasing to *HaShem*. It says in the Talmud[432] that, if sweet honey were to be added to the *ketores*, the world would not be able to tolerate its sweetness. Twice daily we have the opportunity to give this very same offering to *HaShem* in our heartfelt prayers before *Pesukay Dezimra* during *Shacharis* and before *Ashrei* at *Mincha*[433] prayers. We may not have the secret *malas ashan*, but we do have the sincerity of our heartfelt prayers to *HaShem*, which replaces this special spice. The *ketores* was the first offering every morning; it opened the gates for the *tamid* and the lighting of the *menorah* that followed. It can open up the gates of Heaven for you too, so do not take this prayer lightly. Its power is to sweeten your entire life, the same as its aroma once filled the hillsides of Jerusalem for miles and miles every morning. If you close your eyes, you can smell it even today because *Chazal* has taught us that the *karbonos*, offerings on the holy altar have now been replaced by our heartfelt prayers. Therefore, just recite the holy *ketores* with all the love in your heart and the gates will open for you.

Do not pray for your personal needs, for then your prayer will not be accepted. Rather, when you want to pray, do so for the heaviness of the Head. For whatever you lack, the *Shechinah*, Divine Presence, also lacks. This is because man is a "portion of *HaShem* from on high." Whatever any part lacks also lacks in the whole, and the whole feels the lack of the part. Therefore, you should pray for the needs of the whole.[434]

When you want to pray to *HaShem* for something, meditate on your soul as part of the *Shechinah*, Divine Presence. You should have faith that your prayer will benefit the Divine Presence. Then, if you are appropriately attached to the Divine Presence, this influence will also be transmitted to you. When a person is joyous, he unconsciously claps his hands. This is because his happiness spreads through his entire body. The same is true of the Divine Presence. Every influence is transmitted to each of its parts.[435]

The Talmud[436] teaches us that if you pray for another person who is lacking what you are lacking, you will be answered first. Raba said to Rabbah bar Mari: "Where can we derive the lesson that our *rabbis* taught us, that that whoever prays (to *HaShem*) for mercy on behalf of his friend, while he himself is in need of the same thing, he will be answered first? Rabbah bar Mari replied that we can derive that from the verse, "and G-d changed the fortune of Iyov[437] when he prayed for his friends."[438] Raba replied to

432 Yerushalmi, Yoma
433 Afternoon prayer service
434 Lekutim Yekarim #224, Tzavaas HaRivash #73
435 Maggid Devarav LeYakkov #66
436 Baba Kama 92a
437 Job

Rabbah bar Mari, "You say it is from that verse, but I say it is from this verse, [439] 'and Abraham prayed to G-d and G-d healed Avimelech, his wife, and his maidservants and they bore children.' Immediately after that it says,[440] 'and G-d remembered Sarah as he had said… and Sarah conceived and bore Abraham a son in his old age.' Many times, when you're thinking how to help your friend, you suddenly figure out the answer to your own troubles. You would be surprised how many people you know are stumbling on the same barriers as you."

There is an unbelievable story about one of the great *rebbe*s towards the end of the war. The Nazis, *yemach shemom*, told the Jews they were taking them to a beautiful vacation place. Everyone ran around excited, thinking it was for real. While all this was happening, there was one rabbi in the corner, praying with his *siddur*. Suddenly everyone was pushed into the train, even the *rabbi*, but reluctantly one Nazi lifted him off. It was just them standing there as the train started leaving. The Nazi turned and told him, "I want you to know that I watched you. Everyone was taking care of his or her physical needs. You, on the other hand, were standing in a corner and praying. Do you know that when you pray, *HaShem* always answers?" Then the Nazi just quickly ran off [I ask you, was this man a real Nazi or Eliyahu *Hanavi* disguising himself to save this holy Jew?]."

"May *HaShem* open my lips and my mouth will tell your praise." We have to pray to *HaShem* to open up our hearts, so we should be able to pray with all our hearts. The Mishnah tells us that the pious people of yore would meditate for an hour before praying, in order to achieve a proper state of mind.[441] With all the distractions of today's generation, how much more important is the concept of prior preparation for prayer than ever before. Today we go straight from checking our phone messages to praying to *HaShem*.

Rebbe Nachman says, "Prayer and Torah go hand in hand." [442]You can't expect your prayers to be answered if you don't prepare yourself with Torah study before and after praying. There must be a balance between the two, as both are interdependent one on the other and give each other strength. Many sages disagreed over which has precedence, Torah study or prayer. Choosing the middle ground, Rebbe Nachman always remarked, "Pray, study, pray and study some more."

TEFILAH FOR KAVANAH

---

438 Iyov / Job 42:10
439 Genesis 20:17
440 Genesis 21:1-2
441 Berachos 30b
442 Likutey Maharan I, 1

Even though I am dust and ashes compared to You, HaShem, You still find time to hear my supplications. Though millions of Jews are seeking You, You listen and welcome everyone's prayers. Many of us praise you but all the praise in the world falls short, as no being can comprehend what you do for him every second.

Praying is an easy action; all I have to do is open my mouth. To open my heart, though, to truly pray to You, that is something much higher. It is something I need to work on constantly as my prayers are said usually by rote, without concentration. HaShem, please help to make my prayers pleasing before You, to make them true and real from the depths of my heart.

When attacked by outside thoughts during prayer, help me cast them aside, elevating them back to their source above. Help me to not be discouraged when my prayers seem not to be answered the way I want. Help me realize that You are the one who truly knows what is best for me.

Assist me HaShem in praying with humility and negating myself. Help me during prayers to always remember my fellow Jews, who are also suffering, and the pains of the Divine Presence. Let my prayer instill in me emunah and a true change in my character. Help me make a proper balance between <u>Torah</u> study and prayer.

HaShem, without you I am nothing. You give sustenance even to the lowest beasts. I am a Jew and my neshamah is holy. Help me draw close to You through prayer and have the feeling of wholeness of soul. Thank you for all the love You give me, all the hope You bestow on me, and for giving me the ability to communicate to You.

CHAPTER 9: LEKAVOD SHABBOS

"The Shabbos sensation is a sign of the future when HaShem and man will be in complete harmony." (Reishis Chochmah, Shaar Hakedushah 3)

According to the law, when approaching a stop sign while driving, you are to come to a complete stop even if the road is clear. Most of us though continue to roll without completely stopping. If we were to enter that same intersection and see a police car nearby, we would be careful to stop as we should. Many of us enter *Shabbos* rolling through the stop sign, not coming to a complete stop. *HaShem* is watching to see if we collide the past week with the coming week, or do we stop for *Shabbos* properly? The question is, though, how are we in our busy lifestyle to stop suddenly and just tune out the surrounding world? How can we make our *Shabbos* better to get the most of it?

There are thirty-nine types of work we are not allowed to do on the seventh day. Violation of even one can be compared to rolling through a stop sign. Understanding the laws of *Shabbos* to perform them perfectly takes a lifetime of study and practice. We should never assume that we can observe them without a flaw. Our Creator is watching us continually, and every act done on *Shabbos* is noted in its entirety. For our conduct to be impeccable we must develop a respect for this holy day. To accomplish this, we must learn why it is so holy.

"What was created when *HaShem* rested: Contentment, peace of mind, tranquility and restful bliss,"[443] We too can tap into this harmony by resting on this precious day. As much as we unwind physically on this day of rest, spiritually we awaken.

There was a young man who heard wonderful things about the land of Israel and how a person can experience great holiness by going there. After a few months of soul-searching in the holy land, he felt

---

443 Bereshis Rabbah 10:12

concerned as to why he didn't feel the surge of sublimity he had expected. He traveled to the Kotel and to many graves of holy *tzaddikim*. Finally, he approached a *rabbi* and said, "People told me I would feel holiness here, but I feel nothing at all. I'm going to return home disappointed."

The *rabbi* responded, "Do you know what a bafutstick is? Can you feel a bafutstick?" The puzzled young man answered back, "I do not know what a bafutstick is." The *rabbi* responded, "...and do you know what holy is? Come into my *yeshivah* and learn what holy is!"[444] The same can be true of the *Shabbos*. The immense *kedushah* that *Shabbos* brings takes much effort and patience to experience. It is not accomplished overnight. If you want to know what it is to feel this holiness you have to learn about it in great depth.

A king once told his friend the prime minister, "I see in the stars that whoever eats any wheat that grows this year will become mad. What do you suggest I do?" The prime minister replied, "We should put aside enough wheat so that we ourselves will not eat from the tainted harvest." The king answered, "But if we alone are the sane ones, and the rest of the world is mad, then everyone will consider us the mad ones. It is not possible to put aside enough wheat for everyone, so we too must eat this year's grain. But let us make a mark on our foreheads so at least we should know that we are mad. I will look at your forehead, you will look at mine and, seeing this sign, we will know that we are both mad."[445]

Today we live amongst the nations, exiled from our homeland, and as we all know the world has gone mad. Children are now capable of killing, immorality is everywhere, and homes are broken by an alarming divorce rate. It is hard to escape the madness as *tumah*[446] has managed to seep into even the smallest crevices. We as Jews have a special sign that keeps us apart from the madness. This sign is that we are Jews and, even amidst all this insanity, we still remain holy Jews by observing the *Shabbos*. *Shabbos* has given our people a sense of family and has separated us from the *goyim*. "The *Shabbos* sensation is a sign of the future when *HaShem* and man will be in complete harmony."[447]

HaShem wanted to make the Jewish people worthy of the World to Come, therefore; He gave us the Torah and commandments.[448] He also wanted to give us a taste of the spiritual bliss of the next world, so He gave us *Shabbos*. The pleasure one feels on the *Shabbos* is a counterpart of the World to Come, and every Jew can experience spiritual delight on the *Shabbos*.

---

444 Heard in a shiur by Rabbi Moshe Meir Weiss
445 Rebbe Nachman's Stories
446 Impurity
447 Reishis Chochmah, Shaar Hakedushahh 3
448 Makkos 3:16

Chazal have taught us, "Reward for the commandments does not exist in this world." If this is true, then a question arises: how can a person enjoy *Shabbos*? The answer is that *HaShem* in his absolute kindness gave it to us as a free gift. The reward for the commandments may not exist in this world but *HaShem* lets us take pleasure in it, even in this world. We know that *Shabbos* is likened to the World to Come: the Talmud states, "*Shabbos* is one sixtieth of the World to Come."[449] Therefore *HaShem* wanted us to taste of the splendor of *Olam Habah*, as an incentive to do his will and keep the *Shabbos*. "You shall keep the *Shabbos* [for it is a sign... that I am G-d who makes you holy]."[450] If you keep the *Shabbos*, you will experience the spiritual joy of the World to Come; the *Shabbos* will bring holiness into your life. *Shabbos* is, therefore, a "sign" leading to the future reward. This is why it says, "It is a sign.... that I am G-d, who makes you holy." Through observing the *Shabbos*, you will come to know the G-d who will make you holy in the World of Eternity-- in the world where all is *Shabbos*.[451]

When *HaShem* created the world, it was like a body without a soul. Just as *HaShem* infused life into the nostrils of man and gave him a soul, so too he brought the peace of *Shabbos* into the world. It is thus written, "On the seventh day he rested and was refreshed, *vayinafash*."[452] The word *vayinafash* is related to the word *nefesh*, soul, for *Shabbos* is the soul of all Creation.[453]

Each day of the week draws its sustenance from what is done on *Shabbos*. This especially holds true of the three *seudos*, festive meals, we take part in. We learn from *Sha'are Orah* that *Shabbos* is the source for all of the blessing and holiness given to us. Someone who keeps *Shabbos* in accordance with its laws becomes a throne for the heavenly constellation of *HaShem*, blessed be he. Therefore, *Shabbos* is known as *menuchah* (a resting place). As it says in Psalms, "This is my resting place forever and ever."[454] Anyone who keeps *Shabbos* in accordance with its laws fulfills the Torah in its entirety." We also see this in Isaiah where it says, "Happy is the one who does this; he who keeps the *Shabbos* and does not profane it."[455]

The *Shabbos* is the light of the eyes that illuminate the Holy Temple and the world. This is why those who keep the *Shabbos* will have their eyes opened and will have the power to ascertain how far they have reached in their spiritual journey. They will be able to repent for their failings and come to recognize *HaShem's* true greatness. They will be drawn to the

---

449 Berachos 57b
450 Exodus 3:13
451 Kedushahs Levi, Ki Thisa p. 162
452 Exedus 31:17
453 Toldos Yaakov Yosef, Hakdama
454 Psalms 132:14
455 Isaiah 56:2

innermost aspect of truth, to the true *tzaddik* and to those with a genuine fear of Heaven. It will be as if they are engaged in rebuilding the Holy Temple.[456]

The seventh day, being *Shabbos*, is a day of rest from all toil and worldly matters. We should use this day to reflect on the past week and analyze all of our deeds and intentions. It is a time for families to sit down together and draw closer. The *Shabbos* day is truly a present from *HaShem* and is the best thing that can happen to the family. Body and soul are fused, and thereby depend on each other. All week our bodies are stressed from the pressures of work and material matters. We do not have any time to scrutinize what is truly important: our family, friends, spirituality, and Judaism. When *Shabbos* comes the world disappears, leaving heavenly ecstasy.

When a person brings the light of *Shabbos* into his life, it opens up many new doors. The more elevated state you reach on *Shabbos,* the closer to *HaShem* you will feel. Giving your children an upbringing that includes the observance of *Shabbos* is the greatest gift you can give them. Rebbe Nachman said once, "When a person experiences the holiness of the *Shabbos*, he can attain true purity. This means to understand one's own lowliness and to be aware of the greatness of Israel, to such an extent that he is prepared to sacrifice his very life for them as Moses did."[457] Let us teach this *mitzvah* of *Shabbos* to our families and to the entire world.

The purpose of man's creation was that he should strive to emulate *HaShem*. The example for this is the *Shabbos*; the Torah says that you should work six days and rest on the seventh, as *HaShem* did when creating the world. Thus, in the commandment of observing the *Shabbos*, the Torah is instructing us to emulate *HaShem*.[458]

The six days of the week are a preparation for the holiness of *Shabbos*. This can be compared to a man who was sitting in the dark for many days and suddenly walked out into the light. He would not be able to stand the light, for it could harm his eyes. It is the same way with someone whose actions are dark during the week, and he will not be able to receive the light of holiness from *Shabbos*.[459] From this, we see how important it is to make a vessel to contain the *Shabbos*, by increasing one's awareness of *HaShem* and his performance of *mitzvos* during the week.

Rabbi Yudan stated that, according to the tradition of the world, the master tells his servant: "Work for me six days and one day will be for you." *HaShem*, however, says: "Work for your own benefit six days and for me one day."[460]

---

456 Likutey Eitzos 21
457 Likutey Eitzos Shabbos, #12
458 Inner Space p.88
459 Eser Tzachtzachos, P. 55, #44

Shabbos observance is the basis of pure faith. All the charity and other good deeds we do are created with radiance and perfection, only by virtue of the *Shabbos*. This is because *Shabbos* is the embodiment of faith itself. Charity has the strength to bring an abundance of blessings and holy influences, to the world, but they are only expressed in reality because of the *Shabbos*. As the manifestation of faith, *Shabbos* is the fountain of blessings. *Shabbos* brings everything in the world to its greatest perfection. Without *Shabbos* and the faith, it brings, all things are lacking. This relates also to our da'as, the understanding of G-dliness and our knowledge of Torah. True wisdom and the understanding of Torah can thrive only with the influence of *Shabbos* and faith.[461]

As we can see from Rebbe Nachman's words, *Shabbos* enables the actions we do on weekdays to take on a palpable effect. The things we do on the weekdays lack meaning until *Shabbos* comes and adds to their holiness. We too can't experience our true purpose without her. With this realization, it is a wonder that all week long we are not continuously thinking about *Shabbos* and what we can add to make it glorious and holy.

Some people go through *Shabbos* every week and something is just missing. This is because how much you put into *Shabbos* is how much you get back in *ruchnius*. When a person puts into *Shabbos* one day of his week, his *Shabbos* shines double. If he puts in two days, *Shabbos* gives triple illumination, and so forth. When all the days of the week feed into *Shabbos*, preparing for it spiritually or physically, all one's days acquire an essence of *Olam Habah*.

In our daily prayers every morning, when we say the Psalm for the day, we always mention the *Shabbos*: Today is this day of the week of the *Shabbos*. This shows how every day of the week prepares for the coming *Shabbos* and draws holiness from it. Rabbi Asher of Stolin taught that we should look forward to the coming of *Shabbos* the entire week, thinking to ourselves, "When will *Shabbos* come?"[462] Every day of the week, remember the holy *Shabbos* by preparing, if possible, something for its honor.[463]

Once Rabbi Chaim of Tzanz sat at a table on Wednesday at some *mitzvah* meal and he began to speak about the holiness of *Shabbos*. During his speech, he became so ecstatic about it and so full of fervor that he called out to those around him, "*Shabbos* Shalom to you!" It seemed to Rabbi Yuda Tzvi who was sitting with him that *Shabbos* was soon approaching, and he went home to get his white shirt and went right to the *mikvah* in honor of the *Shabbos*. On the way there he met another man who had also been at the table with the Tzanzer and they proceeded together with their

---

460 Pesikta Rabbasi 23:2
461 Likutey Moharan I, 31:2
462 Beit Aharon, Kikkutim, p. 286
463 Derech Chayim 7-42

white shirts under their arms to the *mikvah* for *Shabbos*. When they got there, they saw that they were the only ones at the *mikvah* and then realized their mistake; it was only Wednesday and not Friday afternoon. The fervor of the Tzanzer had affected them to such an extent that they thought *Shabbos* was already upon them.[464]

For many, *Shabbos* afternoon is like a mad rush to get everything done. It is very important that the *Shabbos* be brought into one's home with peace. *Satan* is well aware of the opportunity given him during *Erev Shabbos*. Tempers can easily fly, causing the *Shabbos* to be brought in with accompanying family strife. This is the exact opposite of what the *Shabbos* is supposed to bring. Early preparation is very much the key to avoiding this. It should also not be beneath husbands and boys to take on one or two of the *Shabbos* preparatory chores. After all, if you want to take the light from *Shabbos* you have to put into it yourself. The Gemara says there are three things a man should ask his wife before the arrival of *Shabbos*: Have you set aside tithes; have you put up the *eruv* and have you lit the candles.[465] Rabba bar Rav Huna said, "He must say them in a gentle way, so his family may accept them."[466] Rav Ashi stated that he did this as a manner of common sense. We can see from this that it is very important to keep things calm before *Shabbos*, as much as to get everything done before *Shabbos*. "A man should wake up early [on Friday] to prepare provisions for the *Shabbos*; as it says,[467] 'And it shall come to pass on the sixth day, when they get ready what they have brought in, i.e., as soon as they bring it [early in the morning] it should be prepared [early].'"[468]

"Better a meal of vegetables" - on *Shabbos* - "where there is love [between you and your wife and family] than a fattened ox where there is hate."[469] This teaches you that one should not say, "Let me go out and purchase delicacies for *Shabbos*," knowing full well that he will fight with his wife, his father and mother, and members of his family. "Better a dry crust with peace than a house full of feasting with strife"[470] This pertains both to *Shabbos* and *Yom Tov*; the same concept is reflected in the phrase "*bechibadeso*", "Honor [the *Shabbos*]"[471] - by avoiding arguments[472][473].

All week long we have an internal fight with ourselves, but *Shabbos* comes and makes an inner peace and shalom. For many of us, *Shabbos* gives

464 Pe'er Yitzchak, P. 125, #10
465 Ein Yaakov 139
466 Ibid
467 Exodus 16.5
468 Ayin Yaakov 117
469 Proverbs 15:17
470 Proverbs 17:1
471 Isaiah 58:13
472 Gitten 52a
473 Sefer Chassidim p.35

us the only peace of mind in our life. It is so valuable that, "She is more precious than jewels and nothing compares with her."[474]

Chazal said, "If you prepare on Friday, you will have food on *Shabbos*." One should be very eager to make preparations for *Shabbos*. You should move quickly like a man told that the queen and her entourage are coming to lodge in his house. He says with excitement, "What an honor they are bestowing on me by coming to stay in my house!" He tells his servants to get the house ready. "Sweep, tidy up, and prepare the beds with the finest linens." Then he personally stands in the kitchen to prepare the finest delicacies and buys the richest wines. What greater a guest is there than *Shabbos*, which is called "a queen" and "a delight." How much more that the master of the house himself should take the trouble to prepare like Rava, a leading Talmudic authority, who himself salted a fish in honor of *Shabbos*.[475]

One Friday afternoon, as a new student in the *yeshiva*, young Yaakov Yitzchok entered the yeshiva kitchen and told the one in charge that he likes to personally prepare his fish for *Shabbos*; he picked out a piece of fish, salted it and put it back. The other students standing around laughed at this, saying that this student doesn't know which piece of fish he is going to get on *Shabbos*. The Baal HaTanya witnessed this and realized there is something special about this student, so he tied a piece of string around the fish salted. When they served the fish on *Shabbos*, the Baal HaTanya watched to see what would happen. One by one fish pieces of fish would go around the table. He saw the piece of fish with the string attached placed in front of a student seated right next to Yaakov Yitzchok. The student began to feel nauseous, so he pushed the fish over and told him he could have it. Already, as a young student, he was a "Seer", like his *rebbe* of Lublin.

One is required to get ready cooked foods, meat, oil and good wine for the pleasure of the *Shabbos*.[476]

Emperor Antoninus on one occasion had lunch with Rabbi Yehudah Hanasi on *Shabbos*. Several of the dishes were served cold; nevertheless, the Emperor ate them with delight. He invited himself a second time to partake of lunch. This time he came on a weekday; the dishes were served hot, but the Emperor didn't enjoy them as much. Wondering why this was the case, he thus inquired of his host: "The other meal was more to my taste. Why so?"

Rabbi Yehudah replied, "This feast is without an important ingredient."

The Emperor asked, "Why have you not requested this special

---

474 Proverbs 3:15
475 Sefer Chassidim page 31
476 Beitzah 15b

ingredient from my provisions?"

Rabbi Yehudah responded, "This ingredient is not in your possession; it is the *Shabbos* that is missing. Have you the *Shabbos* in your storehouses?"[477]

Rabbi Chaim Luzzatto said, "The additional amount that you do to honor *Shabbos* and the holidays, the more you will honor the Creator who commanded you to do so. The universal rule is that you should do as much as you can as a demonstration of your respect for *Shabbos*. It says in the Talmud how even the greatest scholars would personally do things to prepare for *Shabbos*. They envisioned what they might do for a prominent person whom they wished to honor, and then they would do the same for *Shabbos*."[478]

Once there was a man who earned the title, "Yosef *Mokir Shabbos*" (Joseph who honors the *Shabbos*). He was rightly called this because, no matter how meager his earnings, he would honor the *Shabbos* with all types of table delicacies, notably the fish. In his neighborhood lived a certain gentile who owned a large amount of property. One day the gentile was consulting his mystic friends and they said that the man called Yosef would consume all his land. Thinking of a way to bypass this fate, he sold all his property and purchased a precious stone with the proceeds, which he placed in his coat. As he was crossing a bridge, a powerful wind blew it off and cast it into the river, whereupon a fish swallowed it up. This very same fish was hauled up by a fisherman and brought to the market on Erev *Shabbos*, towards sunset. "Who will purchase it now?" the fisherman cried in anxiety as *Shabbos* was soon approaching and most people had already cooked their *seudos*. "Take it to Yosef *Mokir Shabbos*," advised the fellow shopkeepers. So, the fisherman took the fish and Yosef *Mokir Shabbos* purchased it. Upon opening it, he found the valuable jewel and sold it for an enormous sum.[479]

Our Sages taught us that, in order to truly observe the *Shabbos* in a holy manner, we must remember and prepare for it all week long. If you see something during the week that you would enjoy on *Shabbos*, by all means, acquire it and set it apart for the *Shabbos* day.[480]

Shammai would constantly eat in honor of the *Shabbos*. If he saw a prime cut of meat he would say, "Let this be for *Shabbos*." If he found a better one, he would place the second in reserve for the *Shabbos* and eat the first. Hillel, on the other hand, adopted a different approach. All his actions expressed the belief in *HaShem* that he would find something worthy for the *Shabbos* day, as it is said: "Blessed be *HaShem*, day by day." It was thus

---

477 Bereshis Rabbah 11:2
478 Consulting the Wise, 6,10
479 Shabbos 119a
480 Beitzah 15b

taught: The school of Shammai says, "From the first day of the week, one should prepare for the *Shabbos*," but the school of Hillel says, "Blessed be *HaShem*, day by day." [481]

If you are able, it is a nice practice to write down something for every day of the week that you will complete in honor of the coming *Shabbos*. See if you can give charity to or personally help an organization that provides the poor or sick with food for *Shabbos*. To make another person's *Shabbos* is a very holy *mitzvah*. Occasionally deliver some flowers *lekavod*, in honor of *Shabbos*, to your friends and neighbors. Think up ideas for yourself in this regard. Make your weekday holy by thinking of the coming *Shabbos* and preparing for it not just for you but for others as well. Teach your fellow Jews about the holiness of *Shabbos* and share this *mitzvah* with them. Rabbi Shlomo Carlebach once said, "If you want to taste the *Shabbos*, give it to someone else." It is such a wonderful thing to see Jews willing to share the *Shabbos* with their fellow Jews. The *Shabbos* guest one invites to stay over or eat the festive meal truly adds to the flavor and *mitzvah* of your *Shabbos*.

One should repeatedly try to take pleasure in the *Shabbos* and festivals. If he is financially insecure, in need all week long, he should take special care to see that there are funds for the *Shabbos* and he should try to enjoy it to the best of his ability. Even if he is prevented from preparing a great deal, so long as he gives it his best effort and his intentions are good, his reward will be like that of a wealthy man who prepares a large *Shabbos* feast.[482]

Rabbi Tachifa, the brother of Rabinia, stated: "The provisions of a person for a full year is determined and set between Rosh Hashanah and Yom Kippur, not including the costs incurred by *Shabbosos* and *Yomim Tovim*[483], and for the tuition of his children in Torah study. If a person spends less for any of these, he is given less; if more, he is granted an additional amount to balance the expenditures."[484]

Rabbi Yochanan said in the name of R. Eliezer ben Reb Shimon that *HaShem* declares, "My children, borrow on my account to better rejoice in the holiness of the *Shabbos* day; trust me and I will repay you!"[485]

Besides actual physical preparations, there are many spiritual practices that can really add to one's *Shabbos*. With all the necessary house chores and physical preparations, it is also important to prepare our souls for the tremendous holiness the *Shabbos* brings upon us. If we are prepared only physically for the *Shabbos*, it just will not be enough. *Shabbos* is much

---

481 Beitzah 16a
482 Rambam, Mishna Torah, Shabbos 30:7-8
483 Festivals
484 Beitzah 15b
485 Ibid

more than a physical day of the week; it's a time when the heavens open up and Divine radiance fills the entire world. We want to be a part of this and feel the *kedushah* in our souls; therefore, we must be spiritually clean. Let me share with you some ways our holy *rabbis* cleansed themselves in order to take on the physical and spiritual change of *Shabbos*.

It is a *halachic* requirement to read the holy scripture of the week, verse by verse, once in Hebrew and twice in *Targum*.[486] Rebbe Nachman explains[487] that the *Targum* language is like a balance beam between good and evil. By reciting the *Targum* and thereby bringing *nogah*[488] into *kedushah*[489], one spiritually purifies himself. This is an important preparation for *Shabbos;* therefore, it is said on Friday.

Rabbi Zev Wolf of Zhitomir related: once the Great Maggid of Mezritch sat in his room, which was next to his *Beis Midrash*, and said the Torah portion of the week, twice Hebrew and once *Targum*. Quite a few of us students were sitting in the *Beis Midrash* [studying] when all of a sudden, a great light shone on us. At once the door of the *Maggid's* room flew open and his flaming countenance was revealed to our eyes. This unusual vision almost caused us to lose our minds. Rabbi Pinchas of Frankfort and his brother Rabbi Shmelke of Nikolsburg; Rabbi Elimelech of Lizensk and his brother Rabbi Zusya of Hanipol, all fled outside. Rabbi Levi Yitzchak of Berditchev went into a state of ecstasy and rolled on the floor under the table. Even I [even though I am not an emotional person] clapped my hands in uncontainable excitement. [490]

Through reading twice Torah and once in *Targum*, an extra soul power comes to a person.[491]

One should be careful not to disrupt his reading of twice Torah and once *Targum* for any conversation, even of Torah, so that he doesn't slacken the taut rope that is trying to sanctify and empower his soul. Having recited the reading of twice Torah and once *Targum*, a person should meditate on repentance because, if you are stuck in impurity, how can you attain to the light of *Shabbos* holiness?[492]

On each holy *Erev Shabbos*, you should meditate on repentance with a broken and remorseful heart. You should feel repentant for all the sins you committed that past week, so you can come into the holy *Shabbos* in a state of holiness and receive the light of the extra soul given to you.[493]

I heard it from my *rav*, the *rabbi* of Barniv, the memory of a *tzaddik*

---

486 Berachos 8a
487 Likutey Moharan 19
488 Intermingled pure and impure spiritual energies
489 Holiness
490 HaMaggid mi-Mezritch, p. 69
491 Yalkut Reuveni quoted in Or ha-Shabbos, p38
492 Or ha-*Shabbos*, p.37
493 Avodah u'Moreh Derech, p.49

for a blessing, and he was told it by an elderly gentleman who was one of the servants in the house of the *Rebbe*, Rabbi Elimelech of Lizensk. The elderly man said, "Erev *Shabbos*, even the men, and women who were servants in the *rebbe's* house, myself included, would beg forgiveness from one another just like on *erev Yom Kippur*. They would all be trembling and crying, and their knees would be knocking against each other until the candles of the holy *Shabbos* were lit. When the candles were finally lit, a great joy fell upon each of us and we all tasted the joy of *Shabbos*, feeling a very great and elevated joy."[494]

By Rabbi Elimelech of Lizensk, every *erev Shabbos* was like Erev Yom Kippur. The entire town got together in the synagogue to say Psalms and they cried and cried and Rav Elimelech would say over inspirational words of mussar to them before the start of *Shabbos*.[495]

The Code of Jewish Law says that it's a *mitzvah* to wash one's entire body with hot water on *erev Shabbos*. If this is not possible, at the very least one should wash his face, hands, and feet.[496]

Why do we wash with hot water *erev Shabbos*? This is parallel to the immersion of the soul in the River of Fire to remove the stains of its sins. So, when you bathe in hot water *erev Shabbos* the stains of your sins are removed.[497]

The *Tosefes Shabbos* [the additional holiness that descends upon a Jew before *Shabbos*] does not cause his countenance to radiate until after immersion [in the *mikvah*, even before midday]. It further relates that the main time for this shining countenance begins after midday; "the closer to *Shabbos*, the greater the revelation." It was also his *minhag* to think, during his first immersion in the *mikvah*, that he is removing the weekday soul and, during the second, to take on the new, extra clean soul of *Shabbos*.[498]

The explanation for going to bathe in the *mikvah erev Shabbos* is: It is a matter of spiritually removing one soul-garment and putting on another. We need to have a different spiritual aspect altogether on *Shabbos*, a different soul-garment. Therefore, we go to the *mikvah*, remove our weekday clothes, go through the transforming experience of the immersion and put on our *Shabbos* clothes, all this being replicated with our spiritual garments.[499]

I asked my father if there was truth to what they say about Rabbi Chayim, that from *erev Shabbos*, after immersing in the *mikvah*, until the end of the holy *Shabbos*, he was a full head taller than during the week. He

---

494 Or Zarua l'Tzaddik, quoted in Or ha-Shabbos, p.48
495 Ohel Elimelech, p. 82, #198
496 Shulchan Aruch 360, 1
497 Taamei ha-Minhagim, p.119
498 Minhagei ha-Arizal, p.31b
499 Pe'er l'Yesharim, p.22a #248

replied, "Son, you know that it's not my manner to exaggerate, and of course I didn't measure his height. But this I can disclose to you, with clear testimony, that I saw him every *erev Shabbos* when he walked to the *mikvah* and as he came back. I can tell you that the man who came back was not the same man. He appeared like a completely different person: his face, his height, and everything about the look of his holy body were altered from what they had been." [500]

For many, a nap before *Shabbos* would be preparatory to their greeting the *Shabbos* queen. Rabbi Tzvi Mendel, the son of Rabbi Zusya of Hanipol, told over an important mashal. "*Tzaddikim* are always progressing higher and higher in their service of HaShem, going from chamber to chamber, ever advancing in the Heavenly Palace, and ascending from World to World. Before they can go forward though, each time they must first shed the life force that they have at present, so as to receive another, greater one. Then they receive a new consciousness and a new perception will shine on them at every elevation. This is the real secret of sleep.[501]

One person who followed this practice was Rabbi Mordechai of Lechovitz, may his merit protect us. He was always careful to take a nap *erev Shabbos*[502], for this is also a component of the honor of *Shabbos*, to receive *Shabbos* with a clear mind and fully alert.[503]

A person would never think of greeting a queen without wearing the best of his wardrobe. The same should be true of greeting the *Shabbos* queen. "Undertake to wear different clothing on *Shabbos*; replace your weekday clothing by putting on *Shabbos* clothes. Happy is the person who has special clothes from top to bottom for *Shabbos*... When getting yourself ready for *Shabbos*... state that you are doing it for the honor of *Shabbos*.[504]

Rabbi Chaim Vital once learned from his teacher the Arizal, "It is improper to wear any of the clothes you wear during the week on the *Shabbos*. The same holds true with the six days of the week. One should not wear any of his *Shabbos* clothing, even his *Shabbos* shirt.[505] Even *HaShem* clothes Himself in a special name (*aleph-heh, raish, riash, yud, aleph, lamid*) in honor of *Shabbos* and it is good to meditate on this name while modestly putting on your *Shabbos* garment.[506]

The main time for giving *tzedakah* is *erev Shabbos* and *erev Yom Tov*.[507] Many women before lighting candles have the custom to give *tzedakah*.[508]

500 Saarei Orah, p.9
501 Menoras Zhav, p.98
502 The day before *Shabbos*, Friday
503 Or ha-Ner, p.11, #1
504 Rabbi Chayim Yosef David Azulai, Avodas ha-Kodesh, Moreh b'Etzba, 4-139
505 Minhagei ha-Arizal, p.33, #15, 16
506 Sharshai Shamos 94, Also see Shar Hagilgulim which replaces the aleph with Zayin in the meditation
507 Derech Chayim, 3-4

On the sacred *Shabbos*, whose deep meaning is the spiritual elevation of all the worlds, the *Shabbos* candle serves to represent the elevation of the soul and of holiness.[509]

There are many customs concerning how many candles a woman should light to welcome in the *Shabbos*. The traditional custom is to light two candles for husband and wife, but many women add one for every child. Some light seven for the seven days of the week; others light ten for the Ten Commandments.[510] There are those who light a *Shabbos* candle in each room that they use on *Shabbos*.[511] The *B'nai Yissachar* told over, "A few of our masters of previous generations were very cautious to always light thirty-six candles, signifying the thirty-six hours that Adam had the benefit of the Divine Light before it was hidden away.[512] This has become the custom of my wife every *Shabbos*. Reb Elazar Mendel lit twenty-six lights, the *gematria*[513] of *HaShem*'s four-letter name. He was careful to use only olive oil, the choicest of all.[514] Most people follow the custom of one candle per member of the household. It is interesting to note though that it says in Ayin Yaakov Shabbos that he who keeps the custom of lighting many lamps [for *Shabbos* and *Yom Tov*] will have scholarly sons. He who is strict in the observance of *mezuzah* will merit a beautiful dwelling. Also, the person who is strict in observing the *Kiddush* [on *Shabbos* and *Yom Tov*] will deserve to have jars filled with wine."[515]

I sat down once with the Kalaver Rebbe. He said to me, "You're the guy that sometimes comes Friday night to my shul." (I didn't know if he really noticed me as there is a huge crowd.) I responded, "Yes *rebbe*, I come with my children watch the *rebbe* dance *boie V'Shalom*." The *rebbe* made a big smile. In the old days, people would travel many miles to see the *rebbe* dance before the *Shabbos* Queen... I have had the privilege to see many great *tzaddikim* dance *kabbalas Shabbos* but if you haven't seen the Kalaver Rebbe dance Friday night, you haven't experienced the way the Baal Shem Tov danced before the *Shechinah* and welcomed the *Shabbos*.

You can really tell how much a person appreciates *Shabbos* by watching them pray the *Kabbalas Shabbos* prayers. This is a period when all the gates are open and that the souls in Heaven pray in unison. It is a period of great revelation and spiritual rejuvenation.

When we proclaim "*Vayechulu*" on *Shabbos*, two angels place their hands on our heads and remove our sins.[516] Then, when a person walks

---

508 Or ha-Shabbos, p.63
509 Divrei Chayim quoted in Or ha-Shabbos, p.61
510 Or ha-Shabbos, p.61
511 Be'er Hativ, quoted in Or ha-Shabbos, p.61
512 Or ha-Shabbos, p.65
513 Numerical equivalent
514 A Chassidic Journey p.112
515 Ayin Yaakov Shabbos 22a

home from *shul* Friday night, he is accompanied by the *malachim*. The sense of *menucha* really starts to manifest itself. What a suitable time to reflect on ways of coming close to *HaShem*. Sometimes this *menucha* is so agreeable that we start to ramble about this and that. The walk home should, therefore, be watched carefully. Torah thoughts and singing are most appropriate for such a walk with accompanying angels. Every week when the Nikelsberger *rebbe* walks home from *shul*, his Chassidim accompany him as he sings aloud in the streets with the joy of *Shabbos*. He also asks one of the young *buchorim* to speak over a *d'var* Torah and together they discuss it. The *Shabbos* walk of *menuchah* henceforth should be carefully appreciated.

Shabbos is holy; *Shabbos* brings peace. The *rebbe* sings on his way home from *shul*. Inner peace; serenity, harmony, bliss; this is what *Shabbos* brings. This is because the peace of *Shabbos* is not only peace between human, but it also instills peace between man and Creation. The Zohar says that the mystery of the *Shabbos* is Unity.[517] On the *Shabbos*, *HaShem* created harmony between himself and the universe. By keeping the *Shabbos*, a person enters into harmony with *HaShem* and the world. Man is then in a state of peace with all of Creation. It is like plugging something into a socket. It has no energy; it doesn't exist until it is plugged in and receives a charge.

During the inauguration of the *Shabbos* (*Kabbalas Shabbos*), prior to the evening service, all universes and observances are elevated. This is the concept of elevation of the universes.[518]

Now that this harmony is in the upper worlds, it is time to draw some down to ourselves through the holy *Kiddush*[519] when we return home from *shul*. It is a custom among the *Sefardim* to call out *l'chayim* after saying *savri maranan*. Rabbi Shlomo Goldman says that this is a practice all of us should keep, as it teaches us an understanding that through our *Kiddush* we get life and sustenance. Therefore, one should have in mind all of his spiritual and physical needs during the *Kiddush*. This is a very important concept to understand. We should make an extra effort to concentrate deeply while saying or listening to the words. This is because all blessing for the entire week comes from the *Kiddush*.

When Reb Dovid of Lelov's *Kiddush* cup reached the Seer in Lublin, he picked up the goblet and suddenly his hand began to tremble. He picked it up and placed it down a few times before he was able to recite *Kiddush* over the cup.[520] It was at this point that he finally understood the greatness of his student.

---

516 Shabbos 119b
517 Zohar 2:135b
518 Maggid Devarav LeYakkov 60
519 Blessing made on a cup of wine
520 A Chassidic Journey p.70

When you recite *Kiddush*, you should: "Make the *Kiddush* with joy, and have the intention that you are giving witness that *HaShem* created the world in six days and rested on the *Shabbos*."[521]

"Six days shall you labor and do all your work." This indicates that, when the *Shabbos* enters, we should feel as if all our work was completed, leaving our minds and bodies completely free."[522]

One should do his best to draw the holiness of *Shabbos* into the six working days of the week and sanctify them as well. The more the weekdays are invested with holiness, the more the forces of evil will be subdued.[523] A person should first perfect his observance of *Shabbos* from sundown to sunset Friday night, until the eve of Saturday. Having already done so, it is a very holy practice to draw the *Shabbos* holiness into your weekday by adding some additional time to your *Shabbos* both before and after. Having personally added time to *Shabbos*, I have noticed my following weekday infused with much more blessing, and material matters go much more smoothly. I, therefore, recommend this practice to those who can fulfill it. It is important to remember quality versus quantity. If extending the *Shabbos* will lead you to use the time wastefully, then it might be better to just end it at the normal hour. Even a couple of minutes at the conclusion of *Shabbos* before *Havdalah*[524] draws a bit more holiness into the weekdays, but how much more so a half hour or an hour. Even when Reb Pinchas Dovid Horowitz was towards the end of his life, he was careful to eat *Melave Malka*.[525] This is because as much as we have to greet the *Shabbos* Queen; we must graciously escort her out at the end of the day.

What is this "rest"? It is the absence of work. It is a recess that is called *Shabbos* (meaning rest). What is this like? A king possessed seven gardens and the middle one contained a fountain coming up from a living source. Three [of his gardens] were at its right, and three at its left. When the fountain performed its duty and overflowed, all the gardens celebrated, saying, "It overflowed for our sake". It watered them and made them grow, while they waited and rested. Are we then to say that it watered the seven? But it is written in Isaiah, "From the east I will bring your seed."[526] This shows that one of [the seven] waters them. We must, therefore, say that it waters the Heart, and the Heart then waters them all.[527]

The Torah begins with the word *bereshis*, "in the beginning." It begins by telling the story of Creation. If you rearrange the letters of the

521 Derech Chayim, 1-41
522 Shemos 20:9, Yalkut Yisro 296
523 Likutey Eitzos Shabbos, #4
524 Prayer to end the *Shabbos*
525 Chassidic Journeys p. 175
526 Isaiah 43, 5
527 Bahir 159

word *bereishis* you have the word *yere Shabbos*, revere the *Shabbos*. The Baal Shem Tov taught: observing the *Shabbos* according to its laws with all their fine points brings the forgiveness of sin.

As a little boy, Rebbe Yisrael of Rizhin was once studying a tractate of *Mishnah* with his private *melamed*[528]. "This tractate deals with a situation where a person for some reason has lost his sense of time and forgotten when *Shabbos* is," the *melamed* explained. "But how can one possibly forget when *Shabbos* is," interrupted the boy. Patiently, the *melamed* presented an example of a man who somehow got lost in a desert and lost all track of time thereby. "Still, it's impossible to forget!" the boy insisted. The *melamed* continued to explain how unpredicted situations could happen. Little Rebbe Yisrael still wouldn't accept any of his explanations. "It's simply impossible to forget," he claimed once again. Finally, the exasperated *melamed* asked him, "Why do you insist that this cannot happen?" The boy responded, "It's quite obvious. On *Shabbos*, the sky looks different than it does all week. When one is in doubt, all he needs to do is gaze up at the sky and he will surely see if it's *Shabbos* or not!"

I'm sure not all of us could see the difference in the clouds between the weekdays and *Shabbos*, but this little boy was able to. Maybe you are able to sense it in another way because there truly is an obvious difference in the world, physically and spiritually.

Rabbi Chaim Zaitchyk said, "The peace and tranquility that are essential ingredients of *Shabbos* should become part of one's personality the entire week. If a person stays with his anger and quarreling, it indicates that he has not integrated the message of *Shabbos*. The tranquility and serenity of *Shabbos* should be so compelling and so deep that it will have a lasting effect on a person's nature. The peace that a person experiences on *Shabbos* should be internalized and its positive effects should be evident in one's relationship with his family, friends, and neighbors."[529]

The *Shabbos* comes from the feminine aspect, this being the central point that draws all six points together. All week long, in our toil to gain spirituality, we are on a male level. On the *Shabbos*, we are on a female level because we can soak up the fruits of all we have done during the week. Hence, a person could labor very hard spiritually all week long, but without the *Shabbos*, he would have no means of receiving it. This is because the *Shabbos* is akin to the final *Heh* of the Tetragrammaton. It is the hand that receives from above. Therefore, without the *Shabbos*, it is like cutting off a person's hand, inhibiting him from receiving spiritually. It is similar to working for something but never receiving it. From this, you can see why the *Shabbos* is of such importance in Judaism.[530]

---

528 Teacher
529 Consulting the Wise, 12, 16
530 Inner Space p.75

Chazal say that when you search for *chametz*, you are supposed to simultaneously search your deeds. The same should be so when you prepare for *Shabbos*. You must search your soul as to how to properly come close to *HaShem*.

If a king offered you a key to his treasure box, would you not take it? For those of us who keep the *Shabbos*, it is difficult to understand how anyone would not accept the key to the treasure from the Master of the World. Then there are those of us who take the key by keeping *Shabbos* in all its laws, but we do not attempt to open the treasure box. For those who go all the way through and open the *Shabbos* for themselves, they discover a light that shines seven days.

It takes six days to prepare oneself physically and spiritually for *Shabbos*. If a person were to prepare five days, then he would not be ready to take on the *Shabbos*. Look at the *Shabbos* as being the center of a circle. As you can see, all six days surround her. How can we not all look at *Shabbos* this way? If only we did, can you imagine? All of our days would be centered on her! This is how *Shabbos* should be in our eyes. The center of our lives!

		Sunday
Wednesday		
Monday	***SHABBOS***	
		Thursday
Tuesday		Friday

Superficially, Creation is characterized by the idea of plurality. The six days of the week parallel the disposition of the six *Sefiros* from *Chesed* to *Yesod*. It is only on the *Shabbos* that the vital unity of Creation is realized. This is when Creation is joined with *HaShem*. The *Shabbos* is therefore called the "Mystery of Unity," when all Creation returns to its Source.[531]

It says in *Shaarei Orah*, you must be precise to fulfill the commandment to eat three meals in honor of the *Shabbos* because it entails unifying very holy things. It unifies this world and the World to Come. The name of *HaShem*, YKVK, is united with its essence, which is the third sphere with the seventh. The three meals on *Shabbos* correspond to the unification of the *Sefiros* (There are ten spiritual *Sefiros HaShem* created that work to keep the world in balance. Every *mitzvah* we do helps these *Sefiros* give a blessing to the world and be balanced again. The world will not be balanced again until *Moshiach* comes. It is our job to fix these Sefiros and we

---

531 *Zohar* 2:135a

do so by following the Torah). The first *seuda* we eat on *Shabbos* corresponds to *HaShem*'s name *Adna*, which becomes one on the *Shabbos*, which is the essence of the seventh *sefirah*'s (*Malchus*) unity. The second *seuda* we eat unifies the name *YKVK* and the third corresponds to *Binah*, which is connected to the essence of *HaShem*'s name *EKYE*. This is the essence of the unity of three, the essence of the verse "and you will call the *Shabbos Oneg*, delight." Therefore, when a person observes the *Shabbos*, desisting from doing labor, and honors it by delighting in the three *seudos*, he becomes a true messenger of *HaShem*. How fortunate you will be to keep *Shabbos*, for you will be a host to the ten *sefiros* (explained in more detail in *Sha'are Orah*).

The penalty for neglecting the three *Shabbos* meals is sickness and disease. The *mitzvah* to eat these meals is part of the basis in celebrating the *Shabbos* with delight (*oneg*). The opposite of "*oneg*" in Hebrew is "*nega*" (plague).[532]

Rabbi Yochanan said in the name of Rabbi Jose, "The person who observes the *Shabbos* with enjoyment will be blessed with boundless inheritance, as it is written[533] "Then shall you find delight in *HaShem*, etc... And I will enable you to enjoy the inheritance of Jacob, your father."[534]

Rabbi Yehudah said in the name of Rab, "The person who observes the *Shabbos* with delight will be granted his heart's desires, for it is said:[535] and delight in *HaShem* and he will give you the wishes of your heart. The meaning of delight is the *Shabbos* given to us by *HaShem*.[536]

On *Shabbos* a person should not say, "Let's go to sleep so that we'll be able to work late on *motzei Shabbos*", since it's forbidden to make plans on *Shabbos* for things to do the next day, even to make plans for writing Torah thoughts. The reason is that this gives the impression that you're resting or sleeping on *Shabbos* for the sake of a weekday. What you should say is, "Let's lie down to rest because today is *Shabbos*."[537]

Studying Torah on *Shabbos* is worth many days of weekday study. This is because a person's mind and heart are open on *Shabbos*. For those who study all week, the *Shabbos* is a time to rejuvenate through eating and drinking. Those that work all week long, *Shabbos* study can make up for an entire week of missed study. During the years I was working seventy hours a week, I found that my excitement to study Torah without the thought of work, carried me through the day with great scholarly accomplishments. I found myself able to study many times the amount of a regular weekday.

---

532 Zohar Eikev 273a, Sefer Yetzirah 2:4
533 Isaiah 58, 14
534 Ayin Yaakov 118
535 Psalms 37, 4
536 Ayin Yaakov 118a
537 Sefer Chassidim, Shabbos p.33

Reb Pinchas MiBrod would not sleep at all the entire *Shabbos* from beginning to end. All night he was bent over his books, studying by the light of a lantern. In the course of the light, he could easily drink twenty-four cups of coffee and inhale a full box of snuff. Once when Reb Pinchas was older, Reb Dovid'l went to the corner merchant to buy the coffee beans and snuff for his father-in-law. When he returned home, he accidentally poured the snuff into the coffee urn and the coffee into the snuff box. Since their colors were quite similar, he didn't notice his mistake.

That night, after the meal, his father-in-law spent the night learning in his usual manner. Drinking his coffee and smelling his snuff, without noticing anything. After *Shabbos*, he asked his son-in-law, "What happened to the snuff this week? It had a funny smell." Reb Dovid'l ran to the study and examined the remnant of the snuff; it smelled like coffee! He then opened the coffee urn; it reeked of tobacco! Sometimes a person can be so involved in his studies that he doesn't notice things of the physical world.[538]

Praying on the *Shabbos* is extra special. The "other side" so to speak is set aside, and there is a manifestation of radiant G-dliness. The prayers of the *Shabbos* are especially beloved on high.[539] The gate of the inner court… shall be closed during the six working days, but on the *Shabbos*, it shall be opened.[540] On the weekdays, prayer needs much more effort than on the *Shabbos,* though we are required to pray every day of the week. If we don't pray during the six days of the week our prayer will simply not work on the *Shabbos.* Also, on the *Shabbos,* our prayers should not be about mundane matters but should rather be focused on our spiritual being and closeness to *HaShem.* This is why in the prayer books the *Shabbos* prayers are completely different from the weekday ones. On *Shabbos,* one must force himself not to think about weekday activities and concerns. The *Shabbos* is a day of rest from all worries and concerns. It is a time to rejuvenate spiritually and physically. It is a true delight if we let it be. We must let go and give ourselves a break and let our minds refocus on the true purpose of life. We must lift up the remaining sparks that have fallen from the beginning of Creation. Our lives should be spent bringing about the final redemption in our generation. The *mitzvah* of keeping *Shabbos* truly has the power to bring redemption into our own lives as well as the entire world. It isn't enough to keep *Shabbos* though; one should live a life of *Shabbos* as discussed above.

---

538 A Journey Into Holiness p. 102
539 Zohar II: 135, III: 243a
540 Ezekiel 46:1

TEFILAH FOR SHABBOS

Shabbos is the greatest gift in the world, HaShem. It is so holy, so precious. Thank You for giving us this special day when our soul shines double. No other nation has Shabbos but ours. What a present you have blessed us with!

Help me to rest and have peace of mind on Shabbos. May I be a vessel to take in all the kedusha Shabbos has to offer to my soul. Let the excitement of Shabbos be appreciated by my family and those around me. Help me to prepare something each day of the week in preparation for the coming Shabbos.

HaShem, please assist me to not be careless with my speech and actions on Shabbos. I want to make the most of this special day to grow spiritually, drawing closer to You. Open my heart and eyes that I should see the kedusha of Shabbos and not be held back by remembering weekday thoughts.

Giving Shabbos to myself is good but help me to taste the Shabbos by giving it to others as well. HaShem, I want to have guests for Shabbos, but the burdens of extra preparations are difficult. Please ease my burden that I can give Shabbos to other people. Help me to participate in hearing the Torah portion and community activities in honor of this precious day.

Thank you, HaShem for this beautiful day of blessing. All our sustenance comes from the three meals and prayers on the Shabbos. Therefore, may the seudos I make, or participate in, be of wholeness and tranquility.

Rebbono Shel Olam, what would I do without the holiness of Shabbos in my life? Thank you for this wonderful and important day of rest. That is, a day to reflect and appreciate all that You have given me. May I keep its laws and observe in the most respectful way.

CHAPTER 10: AHAVAS YISRAEL

The Holy One, blessed be He, said, 'Mmy beloved children, do I lack anything that I have to ask you for it? All I ask is that you love and honor each other, nothing more!" (Tanna de'Bei Eliyahu Rabbah 26)

The root of the word *shalom* - peace - is *shalaim*, which means whole, or complete. Why do people fight against each other? It is because they're not whole or at peace with themselves. "Love your neighbor as yourself," implies not one command but two, in a very specific sequence. Step one, love yourself. This prepares a person for step two, loving others. Animosity towards others is self-hatred turned outward. First, make yourself whole; find inner peace. You will then come to love your neighbor and be at one with your fellow man.[541]

The Nikolsburg Rebbe, one of the greatest *tzaddikim* of this generation, constantly speaks about the importance of *shalom* - peace - among the Jewish people. The Kalaver Rebbe once spoke to me about *shalom,* saying that all the proper pathways arrive at the same destination.

The exploration for peace must be twofold: within the Jewish people, and within each individual. Every person must acquire a harmonious attitude toward life as a whole; so, it makes no difference if things are seemingly good or bad. Such a person will find *HaShem* in everything. Through Torah and the *tzaddikim* we can attain this harmony. Both are called "peace," and through them, everyone can feel his love for *HaShem* - whether things in his life are good or seemingly bad. He will also feel love for his fellow Jew. In this way, peace will extend throughout the Jewish people.[542]

Without loving one's fellow Jew, a person cannot truly love *HaShem.* The Baal Shem Tov used to say that love of the Jewish people is

---

541 The Secrets of Hebrew Words p. 105
542 Likutey Etzos, Peace 6

identical to the love of *HaShem*. "You are children to *HaShem* your Creator."[543] When one loves the father, naturally one loves the father's children.[544] Conversely, "If you do not respect your parents, your children will not respect you."[545]

We all want to feel loved and cared for by others. Many of us are searching for love; whether through marriage, friendship or even a brief encounter in the street. A person's face should always be radiant, and he should receive everyone with a pleasant countenance.[546] It was a known fact that Rabbi Yochanan ben Zakkai always greeted others before they had the opportunity to greet him, even in the marketplace.[547] This was a gesture of *ahavas Yisrael*.

What we need to sustain ourselves emotionally varies with each individual. Some of us need more sympathy, while others need empathy. Much of this should be found within us, but there is a lack of it from those around us. When our reserves of self-love run low, we need to count on those close to us to give us a boost. I've had some days when it seemed that nothing was destined to be right. Even though I made mistakes, *HaShem* was there to hold me. There is no place I can fall that *HaShem* wouldn't be there to pick me up. What is a friend? A friend is someone who is there for you when you need him when it really counts. "Two are better than one, for if one of them falls, the other will lift up his fellow. Woe to the single one, for he has no companion to lift him up."[548] When I am at my lowest point, I don't need someone else to scrutinize my actions. I will recover better with a supportive ear and a verbal pat on the back than with judgment and criticism.

What is *ahavah*? In the literal sense, it means love and endearment, but its true meaning is much deeper than that. The *gematria*[549] of *ahavah* equals 13.[550] The Torah commands us, "Love your neighbor as yourself, I am *HaShem*."[551] Two people who love one another become joined through their love. The *ahavah*, thirteen of one partner, joined with the *ahavah*, thirteen of the other partner, become twenty-six, which equals the *gematria* of *HaShem's* four-letter name *YKVK*.[552] Where man joins his fellow in love, *HaShem* chooses to dwell and make his presence felt.[553]

---

543 Deuteronomy 14:1
544 Hayom Yom, p.81
545 Rambam, Moreh Nevuchim
546 Tomer Devorah 2:7
547 Berachos 17
548 Koheles 4:9-10
549 Numerical value
550 *Aleph*=1, *Hey*=5, *Vet*=2, *Hey*=5
551 Leviticus 19:18
552 *Yod*=10 he=5, *vav*=6 he=5
553 The Secrets of Hebrew Words P. 93

Each of us wants to receive unconditional love with no strings attached! When love is given conditionally, if the condition ceases to exist, the love is gone. Similarly, if the love is not dependent on some other factor, it will always remain.[554] HaShem gives us this love. No matter what we do, he still loves us. "HaShem is good to all, and his mercy is upon all his creatures."[555] We honor HaShem when we show respect to his creatures. Therefore, a person should not abuse any being that exists, for all are made in wisdom.[556] You should not uproot a plant unnecessarily; nor should you kill any living thing without cause.[557]

Unconditional love is what we receive from our parents. It is also what we give to our children. We don't say to our toddler, 'if you're a good boy, then I'll love you.' There may be times when we don't like how our children behave, but they are always confident in our love for them. We all make mistakes. In fact, the Jewish nation has wronged the Creator over and over. Why has HaShem been so patient with us? He does not focus on our errors; he focuses on finding the good of his people. Shouldn't we do the same with our fellow Jews?

What do I want from friendship? I want to know that, no matter what I do, you will never look down on me. Whether I bag groceries or I'm a doctor, I want to know that you will support me. I want you to see into my heart and not be blinded by my exterior. I don't want you to judge me positively just because HaShem blessed me with physical beauty. I don't want you to judge me poorly because I'm overweight or have a disability. I want you to judge the real me; the one inside this superficial covering. Most importantly, I want you to remain my friend, even when we have differences of opinion. We do not always have to like the same things. We can agree to disagree, and still love each other and remain friends.

Rabbi Shlomo Carlebach taught, "The question is not how much you love each other. Rather, the question is how much you love one another when you hate each other."[558] Love cannot be taught; it is a gift from Heaven. We are taught to hate; and this, we must unlearn. Love is the force that binds us with our neighbor, our co-worker, millions of people we've yet to meet (and those whom we will never meet). We learned to love in Heaven before we were born, and we need to return to that pure, untarnished emotion.[559] If we could envision all the people around the world and choose which ones we want to love, would anyone be left out?

---

554 Pirkei Avos 5:19
555 Psalms 145:9
556 Using herbs, animals for food can elevate their being. It is important for kosher animals to be slaughtered according to Jewish traditional laws or it is considered abuse.
557 Tomer Devorah Ch. 3
558 Open Your Hearts, p.15
559 Ibid. p.14

Of course, we have adversaries. Therefore, we learn, "Who is a hero? Who is mighty - he who turns an enemy into a friend."[560]

The real significance of peace is to join opposites. You shouldn't be troubled when you come across someone who is your exact opposite and whose thoughts are contrary to yours. Do not conclude that you'll never be able to live harmoniously. The laws of physics dictate that opposites attract. Similarly, if you see two individuals who are totally different, you should not decide it's impossible to make peace between them. Quite the contrary! Absolute peace is achieved through the effort to make peace between two opposites. *HaShem* makes peace in his high places between fire and water, which are opposing forces. The angels are made of both fire and water yet live in harmony.[561] If fire and water can be at peace, then so can we within ourselves and with others. The pathway to peace is to sanctify the name of *HaShem* through complete self-sacrifice. Then it is possible to pray with genuine devotion.[562]

A *tzaddik* who was not a follower of the Baal Shem Tov was once sitting alone in his study when he heard a knock at the door. "Come in," the *tzaddik* called. A beggar entered with his knapsack on his back. "*Shalom Aleichem*," he greeted the beggar. "What is your name and where do you come from?" The beggar replied, "I am ashes and dust; that is my name. And who are you?" he asked the *tzaddik*. "I too am ashes and dust." The beggar stated," If we are both mere ashes and dust, why must there be controversy between us?" The *tzaddik* understood that his visitor was his now former adversary, none other than the Baal Shem Tov.[563] The holy Baal Shem Tov was saying to his fellow Jew, I don't know how we became enemies. You are supposed to love me because we have one Creator! "Why do people hate one another? Deep down they do not believe *HaShem* created them. If only it was clear to them that there is only one *HaShem* and that he created them, they would love each other."[564]

Rabbi Levi Yitzchok of Berditchev explained, "The Torah completes the verse in *Vayikra* 19:18, 'Love your fellow man,' with the statement, 'I am the A-mighty.' This is to tell us that we should love others as ourselves because we all have one Creator. Therefore, we should feel the happiness of others and empathize with their misfortunes. This is the essence of all of our obligations towards our fellow man."[565]

"Rabbi Akiva had twenty-four thousand students who all died within a brief time because they failed to honor one another properly."[566]

---

560 Avos de R'Noson 23
561 Yerushalmi Talmud
562 Likutey Etzos, Peace 10
563 Sipurei Besht
564 Open your Hearts p.18
565 Consulting the Wise 10:3

Each of the students was a *talmid chacham*[567] in his own right, yet they all lacked respect for the Torah learning of their fellow students. This created a *chillul HaShem*[568] when others saw their lack of *ahavas Yisrael*. They failed to fulfill the expectations for men of their stature and learning. *B'nai Yisrael* merited receiving the Torah because of the *achdus*[569] they displayed at Mount Sinai. We celebrate *Shavuos* when we 're-receive' the Torah every year. Since the students of Rabbi Akiva did not treat each other with respect, they did not merit living until *Shavuos*.

All Jews are kin to one another, for their souls include one another. There is in one soul a component of every other soul and in all other souls a part of this soul. Thus, a person should always wish his fellow well and regard with pleasure any good that comes to his fellow's lot. His friend's honor should be as important to him as his own, for in truth it is his own. It is, for this reason, we were commanded, "Love thy neighbor as thyself[570]."[571]

The Rabbi of Hornosteipel once said, "If any of my *Chassidim* experience pain, even in the tip of his little finger, I feel that pain myself." Rabbi Dovid of Lelov had a son who became gravely ill. The community, who loved the Rabbi and his son dearly, gathered to say *Tehillim* so that he should regain his health. When the young boy showed signs of recovery, they ran to Rabbi Dovid to tell him the good news. Upon hearing the news, he began to cry. Taken aback, they asked him, "The child is so much better; why are you crying"? The *rabbi* responded, "Yes, my son is better because people gathered together, offered up special prayers for him and donated large sums to charity. Let me ask you, what about other people's children? When they become ill, the *shul* is not filled with people praying for their recovery. So why should I not cry?"

Rabbi Dovid of Lelov truly cared about his fellow Jews. He would travel from town to town, going out of his way to greet his brothers and inquire if there was anything he could do for them. He was the owner of a small shop with a meager income. Yet, even in business, his *midos* were impeccable. He was about to open his shop one day when he noticed that, although customers were waiting outside his competitor's store, it was still closed. Rabbi Dovid knew that if he opened his doors the customers would come to him. Therefore, he ran to his competitor's house calling him, "hurry, there are customers at your store." He understood that whatever money was predetermined for him to make would come his way, and he

---

566 Yevamos 62b
567 Torah scholar
568 Desecration
569 Unity
570 Leviticus 19:18
571 Tomer Devorah 1:4

was not going to take advantage of his competitor's oversleeping.[572]

The Chofetz Chaim writes that even if someone does not say or do anything against another person, but merely refuses to talk to him, he violates the prohibition against hating others. Moreover, for every second that one feels hatred toward another person, one violates this prohibition.[573]

"Man can catch sight of his reflection in water only when he bends down close to it. The heart of man, too, must lean toward the heart of his fellow; then it will see itself within his fellow's heart."[574] When so many Jews have fallen, don't you think they are waiting for you to be there for them, to lift them back to *Yiddishkeit*? They are screaming for help; we just don't hear them! They want to know that, when they have fallen from faith and tradition, we still love them. We must show them our love. The Baal Shem Tov once saw one of his followers kiss his little boy. He remarked, "I love the lowest and worst Jew in the world even more than you love your only son." [575]

With so many branches and sects of Judaism in our time, how does a person know where he belongs and how many rituals he should adhere to? This is a difficult question to answer. There is great controversy, not only between the various religions but also within each religion. Judaism isn't just a religion; it's a way of life. We possess a special power to change the world and make a difference in the spiritual realms. We are, after all, G-d's chosen people; with this designation comes responsibility. Being Jewish transcends each of us as individuals and includes all the Jewish people and the entire world. If you have not discovered the special greatness of your soul, you will do so by continuously studying our Torah. Reading this *sefer* or any other that is geared to helping us reach a higher *madrega*[576] is significant to our growth as Jews. As we grow in knowledge and adherence to religious practice, we might think it necessary to separate ourselves from those who are less inclined toward *Yiddishkeit*. This is not necessarily true. Each of us can have a tremendous impact on others. People can see that we are loving, non-judgmental, and live our lives with the *midos* of HaShem.

Still, with so many pathways, how are we to know which one is right for us? We should continuously search, perhaps our entire life, always seeking the best path to follow. There is no one correct course, but there are many that follow the Code of Jewish Law, *halacha*. Some of our greatest sages wrote The Talmud so we would know how to follow the laws of the Torah. From the Talmud, Rabbi Yosef Caro wrote the Shulchan Aruch, followed by many commentaries such as the Mishna Berurah by the

---

572 Not Just Stories p. 134
573 Ahavas Yisrael, ch. 2 & 4
574 Divrei Chassidim
575 Shulchan HaTaho
576 Spiritual level

Chafetz Chaim. *Halacha* is the foundation from which Judaism is built. Every country has laws by which its citizens must abide; we have guidelines ordained by *Chazal*[577]. *Halacha* was not created to add stress to our lives; rather it is a way, the only way, to come close to G-d. Rebbe Nachman says that the Shulchan Aruch is the main work a Jew should learn. Assimilation has affected so much of the Jewish population that most people do not conform with the basic Code of Jewish Law today. The Baal Teshuva movement has returned thousands of Jews from all walks of life, back to their roots. Without a code of law, how would they know what to do?

Rebbe Nachman once said that the Baal Shem Tov achieved the holiness and purity of Moshe Rabbeinu. The Chazon Ish said we relate to the Gaon of Vilna in line with Moshe Rabbeinu. Aren't they sitting in *shalom* together in *Gan Eden* (the Garden of Eden, where our souls go after departing this world)? These were very holy rabbis who, with their diverse ways of serving *HaShem*, remained in compliance with the Code of Jewish Law.

Each of us is *HaShem's* unique creation. Like snowflakes, no two of us are alike. As Jews, we are in the habit of labeling one another. Does the term *Litvish, Chassidish, Yekke,* or *Teimani* define an individual? Are we too stubborn to explore the teachings of those who are different? Rabbi Taub of Baltimore told me that a *Chassidish* man with a short coat in Baltimore could reach a higher *madrega* than one wearing a long coat in Israel. Why must we prejudge? Why must there be even the slightest confrontation and antagonism? Must we look at a *Chassid* with our predetermined notions of what a *Chassid* is like? Shall we view all *Litvish* Jews the same? Each of us is completely unique with special qualities that can be shared with everyone. Germany tore down the dividing wall long ago. We should be seeking similarities that bring us together, rather than differences that tear us apart. It is time we come together with one goal, to bring the *Moshiach*[578]. We must learn to look at one another with righteousness and be *dan l'kaf z'chus* - judge each person favorably.

No one can change the world alone; we must do it together. Let us make a deal: First, we will love each other and together we will show others love. They, in turn, will show more love until it multiplies and reaches everyone. Since it must start someplace, let it be with us, especially from the example we set for our children. A child cannot learn *ahavas Yisrael* when he does not understand why his parents constantly fight. The real victims of divorce are the children who grow up in broken homes. How are they supposed to learn respect for others when their parents do not treat each other with respect? How are these same kids supposed to understand love when they don't live in a loving environment? Children live what they learn.

---

577 Our Sages
578 Messiah

If they learn only how to hate when at home, what will they bring into the world? Where there is peace in the home, the *Shechinah* resides.

It is very important not to forget the honor due to one's parents. "Honor your father and mother so that your days may be long on the land that *HaShem* your G-d gives to you."[579] As a young man, Rabbi Leib of Kelm once came home very late at night from the *bais medrash*. His parents had already gone to bed and he didn't have a key with him. So as not to wake them, he remained in the street all night despite the extreme cold.[580] If you fail to properly honor your parents, your respect for *rabbanim* will be lacking. We learn that there are three partners in a man's creation: his father, his mother, and *HaShem*. *Chazal* taught that when a man honors his parents it is as if he honors *HaShem* and brings the *Shechinah* to dwell with them. Conversely, whenever a man's actions cause his parents to grieve, *HaShem* withholds his Presence to avoid being grieved as well."[581]

One should treat one's *rebbeim* with the utmost respect. One should show appreciation for their time, advice and Torah learning. Some *rebbes* humble themselves more than usual to be friendly; it is vital that you take special care not to treat them as you would a peer. You should respect them for their Torah learning and *daas*[582]. Sefer Chasidim says, "Included in the *mitzvah* of loving *HaShem* is the *mitzvah* of loving a <u>Torah</u> scholar who studies the word of *HaShem*." The Talmud says, "A person who loves a Torah scholar will be blessed with children who will be Torah scholars."[583] Rabbi Scheinberg entered the *bais medrash* one day and everyone stood up. He motioned to them to sit, but my friend was told he could continue to stand. When asked why, Rabbi Scheinberg replied, "When you stand up, you are honoring me for my Torah learning while they are standing to show me honor."

We can learn a great deal about love and respect from *tzaddikim*. There are fifteen characteristics stated of a Torah scholar: stately in approach, saintly in sitting, subtle in wisdom, wise in action, knowing his place, rejoicing in his lot, not according credit to himself, absorbing [in intellect], retentive, reflective, asking and answering, listening and adding [something new] to each matter [under discussion], attending the sages, and learning for the sake of doing.[584]

A single person tends to look for a marriage partner like him or herself. A real *zivug* is a match between opposites. The purpose of marriage is to grow with your partner. You can't grow if you don't see what is

---

579 Shemos 20:12
580 Chayai Hamussar, Vol. 2, p.38
581 Kiddushin 31a
582 Knowledge and understanding
583 Shabbos 23b
584 Derech Eretz Zuta 5:6

missing inside you. The job of your partner is to help you find what you cannot see. Pushing, pulling, yelling, and putting your partner down aren't the ways to show someone the need for improvement. You have to use tact, brilliance and, most of all, love. One must also be patient, as no one can change overnight. Furthermore, while your partner is incorporating your suggested changes into his being, he is helping you discover your shortcomings too. To properly appreciate a spouse or friend, you need time out to reflect. Every day your spouse does hundreds of things for you that you don't notice or appreciate. Especially when two people have been together a long time, they begin to take these small, unnoticed favors for granted. As a result, they take their mate for granted. We have to stop regularly and take notice. Just as we learn to thank *HaShem* for what he does for us, we have to appreciate our partner in life. On returning from *shul* Friday night, Rabbi Simcha Zissel Ziv would not enter his home immediately but rather would pause by the window and gaze at the set table and pleasant food his wife had prepared. He did this to feel grateful for all she had done for him.[585]

While a couple is meant to help each other grow and improve, constantly correcting someone leads to an acrimonious relationship. The most successful technique is to change your own ways and your partner will naturally do the same. If you don't want *chas v'shalom* a divorce, first improve your own *midos*; with patience, your spouse will want to please you back. It is important for *ahavas Yisrael* to start in the home. If you cannot properly love your spouse and treat her with respect, you are fooling yourself if you think you're treating others well. True *chesed* begins at home and extends beyond.

Rabbi Yisroel Salanter said that, when he first started learning mussar, he became angry at the world but remained at peace within. As he studied further, he also became angry with himself. Finally, only the self-anger remained while his anger for others melted away; he became *dan l'kaf zchus* - judging others favorably. [586]

Rabbi Levi Yitzchak of Berditchev spotted a man greasing the wheels of his wagon while wearing his *tallis* and *tefillin*. Instead of being furious at this sacrilege, the rabbi turned his eyes towards Heaven and proclaimed, "See, Master of the World, how holy your children are! Even when engaged in greasing his wheels, he nevertheless remembers to pray to you." The person who judges his neighbor on the scale of merit is himself judged favorably [by *HaShem*]."[587] Reb Levi Yitzchok trained himself to be *dan l'kaf z'chus* – to judge everyone positively. However, favorable judgment by an onlooker does not diminish the error made by a person who misuses

585 Tnuas Hamussar, vol. 2, p.45
586 Ohr Mamussar, vol. 1, p. 55
587 Shabbos 127b

objects of *kedushah*, (holiness), such as a man who wears *tallis* and *tefillin* when he attends to everyday, common activities.

In marriage or friendship, the key to any relationship is giving without the thought of receiving back. The same holds true with *ahavas Yisrael*. If you want to feel loved by your fellow Jews, you have to give to them. The thought may occur to you: what if they don't give back to me? Give to them anyway and *HaShem* will reward you in return. There are so many Jews out there waiting for someone to give them love in the simplest form.

We must work on acquiring sensitivity toward other people since it does not come naturally.[588] The Chazon Ish once advised, "For a person to feel the suffering of others, he must first train himself to do everything he can to help them and to save them from suffering. These types of actions will affect his emotions. In addition, he should pray for the welfare of others even if he does not actually feel their anguish initially."[589]

During the Passover *seder*, one of Rabbi Akiva Eiger's guests accidentally spilled some wine on the tablecloth. Perceiving his guest's embarrassment, Rabbi Akiva Eiger discreetly shook the table so that his cup of wine also tumbled over. "It looks like something must be wrong with the table. It's not standing properly," Rabbi Eiger explained.[590]

Rabbi Yechuzkail Levenstein explains true *chesed* toward one's fellow: "A person who has a love for wealth will persistently look for ways to obtain more money. So, too, when you acquire the trait of loving to do *chesed*, you will look for every possible occasion to do *chesed*. Even though other people could do the same acts of kindness, know that you personally gain when you do *chesed*, and therefore you will want to do all you possibly can for others. Be concerned about the welfare of others even when they do not look for you to assist them. Be motivated to do *chesed* because of an inner desire to help others. "Likewise, loving to do *chesed* means you will not find fault with the recipient of the *chesed*. Since you recognize it is your own need and desire to do acts of kindness, you will not be concerned whether the person could have done something for himself. Your love of *chesed* gives you gratitude for each opportunity to do an act of kindness."[591]

Reb Shlomo Carlebach once said, "Often I mention holy beggars, but people ask me who, *mamish* is really a holy beggar? Open your hearts my most beautiful *chaverim*[592]. A holy beggar is someone who is begging to allow you to give!" If your ears are not open to the cries of the poor, then your ears are deaf, and you will not be able to hear *HaShem* calling either." Reb

---

588 Chochmah Umussar, vol 1, p.11
589 Kovetz Igros Chazon Ish, vol. 1, 123
590 Tzintzenes Haman, p.138
591 Consulting the Wise 11:31
592 Friends

Shlomo was one of the most famous singers in Jewish history, making thousands of dollars per concert. When he died, he was penniless. People even had to collect to pay his funeral expenses. His entire life was devoted to the people and he gave all his money away.

Peace is among the greatest of qualities; it is one of the names of *HaShem*. Wherever you find peace, fear of Heaven is found; where there is no peace, there is no fear of Heaven."[593] Each person who loves peace and pursues it will merit and witness the coming of *Moshiach* who, at his arrival, will initiate with peace, as it is written: "How comely upon the mountains are the feet of the herald, announcing peace!"[594] Our sages of blessed memory declared, "The only vessel for holding blessings is peace, as it is written: 'HaShem will give strength to his people and *HaShem* will bless his people with peace.[595]"[596]

Through practicing what you have learned in *Kavanos Halev*, you will acquire peace. With *HaShem's* help, you should be able to pursue peace between yourself, your fellow man and *HaShem*. For it is through the power of peace that the world endures.[597]

I believe that you can fulfill all of your goals and desires to serve *HaShem* properly. After all, "The thing is very close to you, in your mouth and in your heart to do it."[598] All of the *mussar sefarim* are useless unless you want to implement true change in yourself. Few are man's days under the sun. The time is now, with love.

---

593 Rabbeinu Yechiel, The Book of Middos, Peace P.332
594 Isaiah 52:7
595 Psalms 29:11
596 Yerushalmi Berachos 2:4
597 The Book of Middos, Peace p.337
598 Deuteronomy 3:14

TEFILAH FOR AHAVAS YISRAEL

Ribbono Shel Olam, no being can ever comprehend the chesed You do for Your creations every moment. I am just one of the many whom you have treated with an enormous amount of mercy. For this, I am truly grateful.

I want to imitate this middah of kindliness that you possess, HaShem, to the best of my ability. I want the performance of chesed to be a natural part of my being so that I do so without even thinking. Not only this, HaShem, but I want to literally crave doing mitzvos of this kind.

Master of the world, let me not fall into the trap of judging others negatively, whether it be my spouse, friend or a stranger. Help me to see only the good in others. Help me to see the subtle contrasts, not just in black and white. All Jews are important and there is a spark of holiness in each and every one of us. Please open my eyes and heart to this.

Thank You once again, HaShem for encouraging us to love our fellow man. There is nothing in the world more important to me than to serve you righteously. Even though I am not worthy, you have treated me with so much love and understanding.

CHAPTER 11: KAVANOS HALEV

"The whole earth is filled with His glory." (Yishayah 6:3)

Everyone wants to be an important and special Jew. You don't have to be the most learned and holy person to be important to *HaShem*. *HaShem's* desire is that you attach to Him always. It is the *kavanos halev*, the intentions in your heart that make you real. This heartfelt state of mind is the purest form of praise to *HaShem*.

To be connected to *HaShem* is the greatest enjoyment. No longer do you worry about material problems in your life; you realize that everything goes according to *HaShem*'s plan. Rabbi Pinchas of Koretz said, "When you believe that everything is from *HaShem*, blessed be He, then there is no evil or bad at all - there is just all good."[599]

Living your life without feeling a personal connection to *HaShem* can make you miserable. The Jewish soul isn't supposed to exist apart from the emanating light that sustains it. Depression, anxiety, and worries all stem from separation. It is this separation that we must work on rekindling, for it is our purpose in existing.

When a person transgresses a commandment, he is placing a small article in the way of the G-dly light streaming down to him. After transgressing yet another commandment, he puts another article in the channels of light, causing a separation of his soul from G-Dliness. Feeling an absence of closeness to *HaShem*, he then falls further into transgression, thinking there is no G-d sustaining him. The channel is almost completely blocked up and only a small light remains.

If *chas-v'shalom*[600], Heaven forbid, this is your state of mind at this moment, then search for that small light. When you find it, think the happy thought that you are a Jew, and then think of all the virtuous deeds you have done in your life. Only in a state of happiness can you remove these

---

599 Tosefta l'Midrash Pinchas, #187
600 G-d forbid

obstructions caused by your sins. One by one, repent for each deed, seeking out the first evidence of sin in each matter. Slowly the small light connecting you to your source above will increase, becoming larger and larger. The barriers created by your sins will be removed. You will then be a free man. Once again you are connected to *HaShem*.

Clearing the channels between your soul and *HaShem* should be repeated nightly before you retire to sleep. Your sins must be constantly before you as King David says, "My sin I acknowledge to You, and my iniquity I do not hide."

Besides making sure there are no obstructions blocking the light of holiness, it is also important to draw holy light by performing good deeds. By doing things in order to please *HaShem*, we draw closer to Him. The *mitzvos* are a vital life-force for us. Each *mitzvah* has been designed by *HaShem* to bring us closer to Him and is essential for our soul's well-being.

A necessary aspect of drawing close to *HaShem* is also to nullify one's ego. Without this, it is literally impossible to be close to *HaShem*. He does not want someone to be near Him who thinks too highly of himself. After all, isn't the good action a person does the very reason for having been created: To serve Him with all your heart and body.

The spiritual realms are closed to one who thinks he is someone of importance. We are absolutely nothing compared to *HaShem*. One of the greatest mistakes is to think we have power since everything we have is completely from *HaShem*. If it wasn't for His will, we would not be able to move even a single bone in our body. We must realize that we are only simple beings created to nullify ourselves to His will. The moment we think otherwise, we have separated ourselves from Him significantly.

Another way to draw close to *HaShem* is through mystical intentions, otherwise known as Kabbalah. The entire idea of Kabbalah, Jewish mysticism, is to concentrate on the spiritual and to divest oneself from the physical. In doing so, one can elevate spiritual elements directly. In its simplest form, a person can perform a *mitzvah*, having in mind his love of *HaShem*. In a more complex form, he can concentrate on different letter formations called *yichudim*, unifications.

The practice of *yichudim* uses the Hebrew alphabet as a tool to enter Heavenly realms and consists of various combinations of Divine names. When united in different combinations, these names have the ability to purify spiritual worlds and even change future events. These secrets of the Torah have been handed down one by one, between teacher and student, only circulating among the holiest of sages.

Being that the practice of *yichudim* is too advanced for the average person, the holy Baal Shem Tov and other *rebbes* took these high concepts of attachment to *HaShem* and brought them down to more practical levels for us. Here is one example of what he says, "Whatever you see, remember the Holy One, blessed be He. Thus [when seeing an aspect of] fear, recall the fear of *HaShem*. Even when doing trivial acts, have in mind 'I am separating the bad from the good,' with the good remaining for Divine service. This is the concept of *yichudim*. Similarly, when going to sleep think that your mental faculties go to the Holy One, blessed be He, to be strengthened for the Divine service."[601]

Few of us are on the level of the great *masmidim* who would learn Torah continuously, not even stopping for something to eat. Therefore we, even more so, must work hard to elevate our daily activities to the level of true *avodas HaShem*. Our first reaction when we hear this suggestion is that this is too hard a task to undertake. To attach everything, we do to *HaShem* seems inconceivable. What we don't realize is that this is a rather simple matter. *HaShem* is already shining His light of sustenance upon us always, as mentioned above. We just need to make a direct connection to what we are currently doing, and this leads us to *HaShem*.

The Baal Shem Tov teaches an interesting method for attaching oneself to *HaShem* while dealing with mundane matters. He says, "Attach yourself to the Creator, blessed be He, and in that state of attachment pray for some need of your household, or do or speak something though there is no need for that act or speech. Carry this out in order to train yourself to have your thought connected to the Creator, blessed be He, even when you are occupied in actions or speech relating to material matters, to become habitual to a state of *d'veikus* at that time. [602]

The purpose of Creation was for man to attach himself to his Creator. If it wasn't for this concept, the world would not be in existence. That is how much it meant to *HaShem* to have lesser beings like us to serve Him, to give over His holy *d'vekus*, and share Himself with others. Only His holy nation can reach these states of attachment and closeness to *HaShem*. Happy are we and how good is our portion if we are able to connect ourselves at all times to this blessing and light.

Some people just assume that attachment to *HaShem* is only during prayer and Torah study. These times are certainly the most logical for bringing us to higher spiritual levels, but the real challenge is connecting during the least practical moments, those devoid of happiness and feelings of accomplishment: for example, the middle of the night when your child is screaming, and you have barely slept. If one sanctifies himself during these times, he can accomplish far more than he thinks. In all difficulties are hidden the most important and holiest sparks, ready for elevation.

If you would tell a normal person that he could experience the *Shechinah*, he might laugh at you. He might quote sources that say it is impossible since the concept seems so far from him. When *HaShem* exiled

---

601 Tzava'at Harivash 22
602 Tzava'at Harivash 81

His children, *Chazal* teach us that He also sent the *Shechinah* to watch over them. The *Shechinah* is not something you see physically but it is nonetheless there. If your soul is pure and sensitive enough, it is even something you can feel.

The Baal Shem Tov remarks, "Think that you look at the *Shechinah*, which is at your side, just as you look at physical objects." [603] He is saying that you should feel the *Shechinah's* presence so strongly that it is something physical to you. In general, a person becomes more sensitive to things as he becomes accustomed to them. We have to work on accustoming ourselves to be more sensitive to our spiritual surroundings.

Rabbi Shmuel of Slonim said, "The explanation why many people do not sense a closeness to *HaShem*, blessed be He, from their Torah study and prayer, is that they have no real continuity in their service of *HaShem*. When they serve *HaShem*, they seem to do so in an off-and-on manner. One minute they become enthused to do something and then they stop-then again, they become enthused and again they stop. If instead, you serve Him, blessed be He, continually, without cease, surely that is when you will feel a real attachment and closeness to Him, blessed be He." [604]

The Maggid of Mezritch says the same thing but in a slightly stronger way: "If you see that someone sometimes serves *HaShem* and sometimes does not, you can be certain that he has never truly served *HaShem* as he should. For, if he had served *HaShem* even on one occasion as he should, he would serve Him continuously." [605]

It would certainly be a shame if we went through our lives never really experiencing even a brief moment of true attachment to *HaShem*. Bearing in mind how difficult it could be for a mere mortal to connect to Him, *HaShem* gave us vehicles to assist us: the *mitzvos*. Therefore, being close to *HaShem* is certainly an attainable goal we all can reach.

It says in the Zohar, "A wooden beam that will not burn should be splintered and it will become aflame." [606] The *mitzvos* are completely attached to *HaShem* because they are His thoughts, His will. By performing a *mitzvah*, we become nullified in His will. When performed with *simcha*, a *mitzvah* becomes a chariot into the highest spiritual avenues.

Reb Elimelech of Lizensk explains that there are two kinds of *tzaddikim* on two levels, one higher than the other: There is a *tzaddik* who serves *HaShem* by means of the *mitzvos* and guards himself from violating, God forbid, any small *mitzvah*. A *tzaddik* like this looks forward to his compensation in the World to Come. However, he is not on the level where, by means of the *mitzvos*, he comes to *d'vekus* with *HaShem*, blessed be

---

603 Ibid 137
604 Divrei Shmuel, p.211, #90
605 Or ha-Emes, p. 48
606 Zohar 3:166b, 168a

He. The second type of *tzaddik* serves *HaShem* with thoughts totally pure and by means of the *mitzvos* cleaves to *HaShem*, blessed be He. A *tzaddik* like this draws to himself the pleasure of the World to Come and enjoys the radiance of the *Shechinah* in this world. He does not need to look forward to the World to Come, for he experiences its splendor in this world. This is similar to what is said in Talmud Berachos, where the *rabbis* bestow the blessing, "May you perceive your reward in your lifetime." That you merit to be such a *tzaddik*, to be in *d'vekus* at all times and experience the delights of the World to Come in your lifetime. [607]

Before leaving this world, the Baal Shem Tov's father said to his little son, "My child, always remember that *HaShem* is with you. Never let this thought leave your mind. Go deeper and deeper into it every hour and every minute, and in every place." [608]

The Rebbe of Peasetzna explained, "Numerous times during the day, at home and outside on the street, reflect, with a broken heart: 'All the world is G-dliness, even the particles of earth underneath my feet, as well as the air I breathe inside me- and the reality of all that exists is G-dliness. Why then have I alone separated myself from all this exalted camp of the *Shechinah*, to be independent unto myself? Master of the World! Bring me close to You, surrounded with all Your blessings, and in complete repentance!" [609]

Elsewhere he says, "But even prior to the time when the illustrious vision [of *HaShem*] is actually revealed to you, where you see that all the world is G-dliness... nevertheless, absorb yourself each day deeper in the thought: I do not see it, but does not *HaShem*'s glory fill the world, and did He not create it from G-dliness? Am I not also filled with G-dliness, and are not even the particles of earth on which I walk [G-dliness]?"

The entire world is included in the holiness of His G-dliness in complete nullification; all that exists does His will. Only I alone, in my own willfulness, have removed myself as a separate thing, distant from Him, blessed be He, to wander outside this great camp of the *Shechinah*.

"By meditating on this constantly, and by fixing it in your mind, then you force this thought on yourself... and it is unforeseeable that through this the holy vision not be revealed in your soul. For by itself this is what your soul continually sees - it is just the body that obscures its holy vision. When you force this thought on your body, contemplating on it continuously, your soul emerges and sees. If not always, at least there will be lofty moments and hours when you will see." [610]

If *HaShem* desired it, He could have created the world to look like a

---

607 Noam Elimelech Terumah, p. 41b
608 Ikkarei Emunah, p.11
609 B'nai Machshavah Tovah, Seder Hadracha v'Klalim, #7
610 B'nai Machshavah Tovah, Seder Emtzai v'Yesod haHevrah, #14

wasteland, a place with few trees, few animals, plants, and flowers. This isn't the case, though; the world is so beautiful and special. There is so much detail in each aspect of Creation. The beauty inherent in a little rose that grows from the ground could be meditated upon for hours. Its color is bright and refreshing. The smell that comes forth is one to dream of, lifting a person's heart to moments of utter bliss. Now if only in our minds we also connected this little flower back to its source of true nourishment, thinking about the Artist who created it so remarkably. There is truly nothing in Creation that cannot be used as a tool to help us draw close to *HaShem* our Creator.

Most of us don't spend our entire day surrounded by the beauty of forests and hills. Still, if we paid more attention, we would see many marvelous wonders that we seem to overlook on a daily basis. When we see a man-made invention, we do not always appreciate that its source is still from *HaShem*. All physical matters in the world contain light and *HaShem* put them before us in order to help us appreciate His glory. Even a little rock on a sandy beach should bring us to a level of *d'vekus* and dance right then and there before our Creator blessed be He. Instead of missing these subtle reminders from *HaShem*, we should open our eyes and take in our surroundings with an open mind.

Being that many of us sit before a computer monitor or behind a desk for a living, the task of connecting our thoughts and actions to *HaShem* might be difficult. However, it is certainly within our grasp. As stated above, it is a good idea to gradually learn how to connect to *HaShem* while doing mundane tasks. Here are some more ideas to help you do so:

At times when you feel separated from *HaShem*, call out in a heartfelt tone: "Master of the World, all I want is to be close to You. Draw me near to You. I cannot bear being separated from You." Do this until you are accustomed to connecting with *HaShem* at all times. As mentioned elsewhere in this *sefer*, it is also helpful to attach yourself to *HaShem* by picturing the holy name of YKVK.

A person should think to himself, "When will I be worthy of the light of the *Shechinah* to dwell within me?" [611] If you yearn for holiness, *HaShem* will assist you in attaining it. Without yearnings of the heart, a person would not feel any life inside him, sensing little purpose to his existence. Therefore, make a commitment that all the yearnings of your heart should be directed towards *HaShem*. Once *HaShem* sees your sincerity, He will lift you up and purify your soul to its very core.

Rabbi Mordechai of Chernobyl taught, "You must sever all your desires and crave for *d'vekus* with the Supernal Light of the Creator, blessed be His name, with love and longing and yearning, until your soul is about to

---

611 Tzavvas ha-Ribash p.2

expire from the sweetness of the *d'vekus*. This should be every minute and second, and you shouldn't cease from this for one minute." [612]

It is a good idea before doing any *mitzvah* or action to state specifically that you are doing this entirely for *HaShem*. This way, a simple task is elevated to greater levels. There are many prayers created by our sages that can be said before performing specific *mitzvos*. If you cannot find these prayers, then feel free to say a few words emanating from your own heart. The main thing is to find a way to elevate as many *mitzvos* in mundane matters as possible, with the purest of intentions.

Through practicing these *kavanos halev*, we will surely turn our hearts in the direction of *HaShem* and completeness. Thus, it would be impossible not to complete our individual tasks in this world, living and breathing every moment as a true servant of *HaShem*, blessed be He. The realization that the "whole world is full of His glory"[613], will become an inherent part of us. Those around us will bask in the light that surrounds us because our direct connection to *HaShem* will be contagious. We will be able to give others from the uniqueness of our souls, helping them also to come close to *HaShem*. Our soul will be pure and in *d'vekus* with *HaShem* as our egos dissipate, allowing only for *HaShem* to lead us. This realness is not dependent on our level of genius; it is the simplicity of being completely nullified in our source. May the *kavanos halev*, meditations of the heart, bring us to a complete and true *avodas HaShem*, allowing us to grow true to our own holy souls, bringing *nachas*, satisfaction to *HaShem*.

---

612 Likkutei Torah, Hadracha 1
613 Yishayah 6:3

PRAYER FOR KAVANOS HALEV

Thank You, HaShem for allowing me, a simple Jew to speak to You about the troubles of my heart. HaShem, I am so distracted by the things of this world that sometimes I forget there is a Creator controlling all the events of my life. I'm so busy with work and daily chores that there is little time to meditate on the purpose of the world. If only I could feel Your nearness, it would mean so much to me and fix all of my anxieties.

I know the sages have told us that we can elevate even our sleep to a level of true devotion to HaShem, but this is something I feel far from. It's almost as if it's so easy to become close to you that I push You away instead. Help me, HaShem, to turn my life around and bring it more realness. Enable me to connect my every action to You in complete sincerity.

Everywhere I look I am able to see Your glory, though I seem to forget to connect my surroundings to You as I should. When I finally take notice, there are times when I still lack the concentration and devotion I should have in being Your servant. Please help me to appreciate the things I have been blessed with, those things I have overlooked and all the happenings of my life. Allow me to reflect before performing the mitzvos, giving them the proper kavanah of my heart.

Thank You, HaShem for all the patience You have had with me, all these years of my life. Thank You for all the times that I was far from You and, nonetheless, you drew me near to You even though I was unworthy. Allow me to complete my soul and to spread the wisdom of our sages to all mankind.

Made in the USA
Columbia, SC
14 September 2018